Travels in the Dordogne

PHOENIX PUBLISHING ASSOCIATES

St. Amand de Coly

Travels in the Dordogne

Fiona Fennell

Phoenix Publishing Associates Ltd.,
Bushey, Herts.

Acknowledgements

My sincere thanks to the many people who have
helped me with this book. The Syndicat
d'Initiative (local tourist offices) who gave me so
much historical information, the Hoteliers and
Restauranteurs who fed me so well and the
Winegrowers who not only let me wander
through their vineyards but kept me very
well oiled. Lastly I would like to say a special
thank you to my dear husband, Innes, who
stood by my side for three solid months, drove
me over 10,000 miles and without whom this
book would not have been possible.

First published in Great Britain in 1987 by
Phoenix Publishing Associates Ltd
14 Vernon Road, Bushey, Herts, WD2 2DL

ISBN 0 946576 78 5

Printed and bound in Great Britain by
Robert Hartnoll (1985) Ltd., Bodmin, Cornwall

Typeset by Margaret Spooner Typesetting
Designed and Produced by Snap! Books
Cover illustration by Malcolm Forrest
Illustrations by Anne Forrest

Contents

Château de Jumilhac

Author's Preface

Innes (my husband) and I bought our first restaurant 'La Candide', named after that wonderful T.V. series 'Secret Army' and specialising in Regional French Cuisine, in early 1982. We could not have wished for more success, into the Michelin Guide in six months and always busy. By 1984 I was writing food articles for glossy magazines, and it was then that I decided to write this book.

Why choose the Dordogne?

Well, I have a childhood memory of stuffing myself luxuriously with Pâté de Foie Gras and everything else on the menu of a wisteria-covered Auberge near Pleaux, and also because the Dordogne is more generally known as a region, not a river, and its source and mouth are often neglected. It is an area of long hot summers, always a good ingredient for a holiday. It is 310 miles long, just right for a two-week vacation, the landscape is so varied, and there are some wonderful places to visit along its course.

The places you will read about and visit in this little travelogue are the towns, villages and monuments which Innes and I particularly liked. It is therefore not intended to be exhaustive of the area.

Why did we choose Saignes as a starting point?

We were looking for a pretty, rural village with old world charm from where we could drive easily up to the mountains to find the source of the river, and by taking a wrong turning we discovered Saignes. This is often the best way of finding glorious places, once the heat of the argument over whose fault it was has subsided. Watch out for 'Belvedere'! Don't be as surprised as I was to find no village at the end of the track. Only later did I discover that it means a view-point.

In the following pages you will first find a general introduction to the Dordogne, to put the area into perspective and explain later references in the Itinerary. Then the Epicure's Guide. Two short sections, one on food and the other on wine to whet your appetite and stimulate the palate. A short section of 'Handy Tips' which may be useful for reference while you are travelling precedes the Itinerary itself, your holiday along one of France's loveliest rivers. After the Itinerary are a selection of recipes from specific hostelries. These are the restaurants where Innes and I enjoyed our meals the best.

My aim is to awaken your determination to visit a region which richly deserves your time.

Bon voyage et bon appetit!

Fiona Fennell

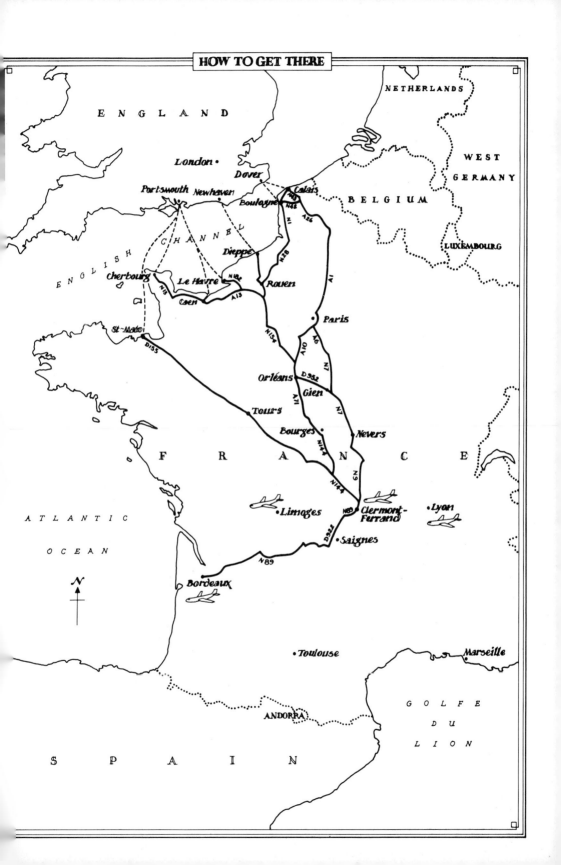

Château Montfort

Introduction To The Dordogne

Pre-history: A Summary

ERA	PERIOD	AGE (millions of years) BP*	LIFE
PRE-CAMBRIAN		4750	Age of planet
		2000	Life begins
PALAEOZOIC	Cambrian	600	Invertebrates
	Ordovician	500	in sea
	Silurian	440	
	Devonian	400	Land plants
	Carboniferous	350	Amphibians
	Permian	270	Mammals, reptiles
MESOZOIC	Triassic	225	
	Jurassic	180	Dinosaurs
	Cretaceous	135	First birds
CAENOZOIC	Eocene	70	
	Oligocene		Molluscs
	Miocene	25	Birds, Mammals
	Pliocene		
	Pleistocene	1	MAN

MAN in the PALEOLITHIC AGE

ERA	CULTURE	REMAINS	CLIMATE
LOWER PALEOLITHIC to 150000 BP	Abbevillian Clactonian	Java Man	Günz Ice Age Warm Period
		Swanscombe Man (England)	Mindel Ice Age Warm Period
	Acheulean	Fontechevade Man (Charente)	Riss Ice Age
MIDDLE PALEOLITHIC to 40000 BP	Tayacian	NEANDERTHAL MAN	Warm Period
	Levalloisian		
		La-Chapelle-aux-Saints Man	Würm Ice Age
		La Ferrassie Man	
	Mousterian	Mousterian Man	
UPPER PALEOLITHIC to 10000 BP	Périgordian Aurignacian	HOMO SAPIENS	
	Solutrian	Grimaldi Man	
		Cro-Magnon Man	
	Magdalenian	Chancelade Man	

* BP — Before Present, conventionally taken to be before 1950.

History and Pre-history

The fertility of the land and the plentitude of rivers have made the Dordogne region a favoured habitation for mankind over the millennia. Indeed the dawning of history in this area marks the earliest we know of mankind — for this region is world-renowned as perhaps the richest source of information on our forefathers in Europe.

Dotted through the caves by the rivers of the Périgord are traces of the cultures which flourished here in the Upper Paleolithic era. At Montferrand, Périgord, Comb Kapelle man was discovered at the turn of this century, he is thought to be a specimen of the very earliest type of Upper Paleolithic in Europe. Cro-Magnon man was found in 1868 in a cave by the village of Les Eyzies. The Cro-Magnon type of men were distinguished by their height, nearly 6ft, and by having strong jaws and neck muscles combined with short, broad faces. It has been said that the Cro-Magnon type can still be found among the inhabitants of the Dordogne — and certainly a surprising number of men in the area seem to fit this physical description.

The Magdalenian Culture — again of the Upper Paleolithic — is named after the cave of La Madeleine in the Dordogne where their tools and carvings were found. The Magdalenian Culture lasted through the arctic weather of the last Ice Age and so the Dordogne can be seen as once inhabited by reindeer hunters and fisher-folk. To this area so rich in pre-historic remains, the most stunning addition was made in 1940 by a boy following his dog into a hole in the hilltops by Montignac. The brightly painted caves of Lascaux that the child discovered have done much to explain the lifestyle of the Dordogne hunters at around 1800 BC. The drawings suggest that the hunters attacked and trapped fast-moving animals whenever a river slowed them down, hence perhaps one reason for the numerous settlements in the area. The Lascaux caves began to deteriorate and so they have been resealed, but an exact replica has been built which is well worth visiting.

Records show that gradually Gaulish tribes settled at Bordeaux, Périgueux and Cahors — and were ousted by the Roman occupation. The Romans, delighted to find such a fertile region, called the area Aquitaine because of the number of rivers — and planted vines around Bordeaux. As the Roman Empire collapsed, chaos came to the area; the Saracens attacked from Spain, Visigoths and Barbarians from the North, and in 848 the Vikings sailed up the rivers to pillage the valley communities. During the eleventh and twelfth centuries peace was gradually restored, until Henry Plantagenet married Eleanor of Aquitaine in 1152 — and became Henry II of England in 1154. For 300 years England ruled the west of France and Bordeaux became their base. Throughout the Dordogne remains inextricably the imprint of English ownership — indeed some of the English monarchs preferred it to England. The Black Prince held his court at Bordeaux from 1356–71, and his eldest son Richard II (the Lionheart) was born in France. Understandably, English ownership was much disputed and gradually the sporadic battles intensified to become the Hundred Years' War — a period whose legacy of battle architecture can be seen the length of the Dordogne. Small towns, bastides, were given ramparts, the towns themselves were arranged in grid and block patterns to allow a swift passage of arms to reinforce positions. The war was primarily a matter of guerilla tactics — across the waters of the Dordogne a French force would surge forth from the castle of Beynac to attack the British stronghold of Castelnaud opposite, and then vice versa.

Finally the English withdrew after suffering a major defeat at the Battle of Castillon in 1453. The French monarchs tried to re-absorb the area, wooing them with a separate Parliament at Bordeaux, a new University... unfortunately these were not felt by many to be adequate compensation for the major loss of business and tax advantages occasioned by the departure of the English.

Further scenes of turbulence came to the area in the next century during the Wars of Religion: battles between Catholic-backed monarchs whose spiritual allegiance gave them the political support of Spain, and the Huguenots (Protestants) based mainly in the South and South-West of France, headed by princes of royal blood with Henri of Navarre in the forefront, and naturally supported by England and sometimes a few Germanic princes. The wars set town against town as each one was taken by opposing armies. In 1598 the Edict of Nantes confirmed Henri of Navarre on the French throne (although now 'converted' to Catholicism) and peace in the region seemed to be close. However, the dispute continued to flare up as Cardinal Richelieu and Louis XIV worked to restrict the power of the Huguenot nobles.

A century later through the length and breadth of the land the Revolution brought widespread death and destruction. Over 18,000 people are known to have perished — more than two-thirds of these were just ordinary workers, not 'aristocrats'. The physical scars left along the Dordogne were the destruction and defacement not only of religious buildings, as in the Wars of Religion, but this time also the castles.

The area's involvement in major conflicts has continued into the twentieth century: in 1917 the first US troops to join the war landed at Bassens. In World War II Bordeaux hosted the French government before the Vichy takeover — and once again the inhabitants of the Dordogne were set against each other, collaborators versus the resistance.

Architecture

This history of struggle and conflict has naturally left its mark on the architecture of the region. Rather than luxuriant châteaux, fortified castles and bastides are the more characteristic landmarks. And there are some splendid ones ranging from the massive Beynac to the more romantic Château de Val near Bort-les-Orgues.

Where there were no castles to protect the land and the people, 'bastides' were built, particularly during the thirteenth century. They were built on free land and were outside the feudal system, their citizens were protected by the town's charter and a serf could free himself from his feudal obligations by living and fighting there for a year and a day. The whole design of the town was geared to defence — strong encircling walls, solid defendable gates, straight streets, even the church would be fortified as the final bastion against invaders. Domme, which is visited on Day 6 of the Itinerary, is a perfect example of this kind of town. Again, at Libourne the grid pattern of streets can be observed, although the ramparts are now tree-lined avenues.

At Blaye such fortifications have their apotheosis in the splendid citadel by Vauban, Louis XIV's military engineer. Finished in 1689, it is enormous — over half a mile in length, it completely obliterated the original medieval town on the site. Inside the ramparts it forms a precisely arranged pattern of moats, towers and huge stone gateways. The soldiers' quarters are regularly arranged

Eymet, showing bastide grid layout

in streets and squares including such necessities as the church and hospital. Impressive, not only in the massiveness of its design but also in its thoroughness, it guards the entrance to the Dordogne and all its riches.

Abbeys and churches suffered most heavily during the centuries of conflict and there are few religious buildings that remain either complete or wholly of one particular period. At Beaulieu-sur-Dordogne the twelfth century church still stands, but the Cluniac monastery which encompassed it has now gone. This serves to make the remaining detail of the sculpted porch a richer and more poignant discovery.

Famous Names

Perhaps the most renowned name often associated with the area is that of Cyrano de Bergerac, he of the long nose and fiery temper. Unfortunately, although his family may have had roots in the Périgord region, Cyrano was known by the name of a family estate called 'Bergerac' in the valley of Chevreuse.

Etienne de la Boetie (1530–63) the humanist, was born at Sarlat. Michel de Montaigne was by him when he died and wrote the famous essay 'On Friendship' to his memory. Montaigne (1533–93), mayor of Bordeaux 1581–85, was born and died at the Château de Montaigne outside Bergerac. Maurice de Biran (1766–1848) the philosopher was born at Bergerac, as was Mounet-Sully the tragedian (1841–1916). Josephine Baker the British music hall star planned to renovate and live at Les Milandes (west of Castelnaud) with her numerous adopted children. Unfortunately the project collapsed and helped to financially ruin her. Just outside Mussidor lies the Château de Mont-Real, the lord of which is said to have gone to Canada — and named the city of Montreal.

From the Bordeaux area the celebrities come thick and fast, this is a small sampling:

Writers: Ausonius — 4th century Roman Poet
Jacques Rivière — (1886–1925)
François Mauriac — (1885–1970)
Jean Anouilh — (1910–)

Musicians: Lamoureux — (1834–99)
           Garat — (1764–1823)
           Jacques Thibaud — (1880–1954)
           Henri Sauget — (1901–)
Artists: Carle Venet — (1758–1835)
           Narcisse Diaz de la Peña — 1807–79)
           Odilon Redon — (1832–82)
           Albert Marquet — (1875–1947)
           Andre Lhote — (1885–1962)

Francisco de Goya (1746–1828) the Spanish painter who escaped from his homeland came to live and die in exile in Bordeaux.

Land Use and Agriculture

Regions of the valley of the Dordogne: its agriculture and produce

Man's chief activity remains the husbanding of the soil

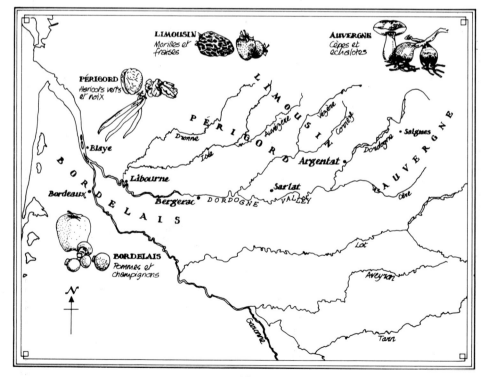

Auvergne (derived from the Gaulish tribal name 'Averni')

Auvergne is first and foremost volcanic in its origins, and therefore it is a varied upland region, an area which is not easy to describe in general terms. The natural woodland was probably beech and this is still the most common tree, although pines have been planted, and sweet chestnut grows well on the Crystalline slopes*. In the valley, where here and there a small volcanic hill breaks the smoothness of the land, the soil is rich. Rye, once universally grown, has largely been replaced by barley, oats, potatoes and increasingly fodder crops.

Areas of pasture are used for stock-rearing, mainly dairy cattle. They are, however, snow-covered for several months of the year, so, the animals move seasonally between villages and farms in the valleys, where they are stall-fed on fodder crops, and the high grazing land. The emphasis is on milk production, although calves for veal are sent to the markets of Paris and Lyon in early summer. Cheese is produced in large quantities, notably the 'fromages bleus' of Auvergne of which two well-known varieties are Fourme d'Ambert and Bleu St. Nectaire. Sheep are less common but what ewe's milk exists is turned into cheese which is processed in Roquefort.

Pigs are reared on a smaller scale and used to make local charcuterie. Warm, sunny slopes in Auvergne are covered with vineyards producing St. Pourçain, and orchards, including cherry trees, whose fruits make the regional tart 'Clafoutis' (see p. 37).

Limousin

At first there are red soils, and green fields full of grazing cattle with cowbells jingling in the wind: lines of oak and chestnut and a sense of being in the depths of rural France. At higher levels the scene changes; above 2,000 ft there is a country of granite hills, a sterile, melancholy land of heather and bracken.

The part of this region which lies to the south and stretches down as far as Argentat is known as Lower Limousin, an area with a delightful variety of landscapes through which you will pass. The large tracts of woodland

* Crystalline slopes: slopes originally formed by the heat and pressure of volcanic movement.

contribute to the economy: both mature timber and coppice provide firewood, constructional timber, wood for barrel-making and vine and hop poles. Oak bark is used in the tanneries, pigs feed on acorns and beechmast, and chestnuts form a supplement to the economy. Arable land occupies a smaller part of this region. Rye and buckwheat are grown on high ground and wheat and barley lower down. Maize (for fodder) is grown where the valley widens towards Argentat on the Dordogne.

The main development in the economy of Limousin is in cattle-rearing for beef and veal. The Limousin cattle are one of the most outstanding French breeds, and the markets in Limoges attract buyers from far afield. Pigs are also reared and large numbers sold off at annual fairs. As in Auvergne a small proportion of vines are grown for local table wines, particularly 'Vin de Glanes'.

Périgord

Périgord corresponds closely to the department of Dordogne. In the early seventies about 36 per cent of the total area was under woodland, 24 per cent under arable cultivation and 19 per cent under permanent pasture. Chestnut trees have long been widespread. Chestnuts (Marrons) are used for human consumption and sent to Bordeaux markets, they are also fed to pigs and even sheep. Several varieties of oaks are found, some growing in woodlands and others in copses on the plateaus or on the valley slopes. For centuries herds of swine have been pannaged in these oak woods. About a foot or so beneath the ground around the oak trees grow the renowned Périgord truffles.

Conifers have been planted since the mid-nineteenth century especially since the 1914–18 war. These woodlands supply construction timber. Almost half the arable land in this area grows cereals; chiefly wheat with some maize (for fodder) and barley.

Cattle and sheep are present and pigs are reared on skimmed milk from the dairies, rather than on acorns and chestnuts in the woods. The breeding of capons, ducks, turkeys and geese is widespread, the fattened and truffle-stuffed birds are sent to Paris markets.

The Périgord is rich in cherries, peaches, greengages and plums, the last especially around Bergerac where they are dried, and in Périgueux where the potent 'Eau-de-Vie de Prunes' is distilled. Unexpectedly, apples are grown for cider-making. Walnuts are grown in groves. Some nuts are crushed for oil, some exported green, others shelled and dried or pickled, while the walnut wood is used for furniture. Perhaps surprisingly, tobacco is grown in large quantities in Périgord. The plant requires assiduous care and a large labour force, but it is a useful addition to the cash income of the smaller farmer.

Finally we come to the vineyards. They produce the wines of Bergerac, Pécharment and Monbazillac: the famous sweet white wine traditionally served with 'Foie Gras'.

Bordelais

This area, although it has its share of cattle, cereals and maize, is primarily a wine region. Bordelais has been a producer of wine for centuries. Production reached 1.3 million hectolitres by 1870, but as a result of Phylloxera* fell to about 0.8 million in succeeding years. Recovery has since been steady, and output has increased to as much as four times more than before the dreaded Phylloxera, and 90 per cent of this is of quality wines.

Many holdings are small: only 3 per cent exceeding 75 acres, and five-sixths of the estates are less than five acres each. The co-operative movement (see p. 42) has grown, especially since 1952. These operate mainly in the districts of high-yield, medium quality wines.

Of the districts in this region through which you will pass — St. Emilion, Pomerol, Fronsac, Côtes de Bourg and Côtes de Blaye — the most famed are St. Emilon and Pomerol, situated near Libourne on the northern side of the Dordogne. These produce considerable quantities of red wine of a heavier quality than claret.

---

* Phylloxera: The Phylloxera is an aphid of American origin which first appeared in Languedoc in 1863, and had spread to the Bordeaux district by 1868. It multiplies prodigiously living in galls on the leaves and roots, where it cannot be reached by spraying. The affected vines become stunted and die. By 1884 the whole of France was affected and no treatment could be found.

In 1891 it was discovered that vine stocks from the eastern U.S.A. were almost immune, and a vast programme of grafting European scions on to these stocks was begun. These vines are not wholly resistant, but are affected much less seriously.

Main Local Produce

PRODUCE	AVAILABILITY	AREA
Vegetables		
CABBAGE — Chou	Autumn and winter	Auvergne
SHALLOT — Echalote	Fresh June/July but available all year	Auvergne
BEANS — Haricots verts	June to October	Périgord
LENTILS — Lentilles	Available all year	Auvergne
POTATOES — Pommes de Terre		
New	Summer	Périgord
Old	Winter	Auvergne
Edible Fungi		
MUSHROOMS		
— Champignons	Available all year	Bordelais
— Cèpes	Autumn	Auvergne, Limousin, Périgord
— Morilles	Spring	Limousin, Périgord
TRUFFLES — Truffes	Winter	Périgord
Fruits		
APPLES — Pommes	August to October	Limousin, Périgord, Bordelais
TOMATOES — Tomates	March to November	Périgord, Bordelais
PLUM — Prune	July onwards	Limousin, Périgord
RASPBERRY — Framboise	June to July	Limousin
STRAWBERRY — Fraise	May to June	Limousin, Périgord
CHERRY — Cerise	June to July	Auvergne, Périgord
GREENGAGE — Reine-Claude	July and August	Périgord
PEACH — Pêche	June to September	Périgord
Nuts		
CHESTNUT — Marron	September to November	Auvergne, Limousin, Périgord
HAZELNUT — Noisette	Autumn	Limousin, Périgord
WALNUT — Noix	September to January	Limousin
	October	Périgord

Traditional truffle hunting in the Périgord

Regional Fungi

TRUFFLES — (La Truffe)
These underground fungi belong to the division of the *Ascomycetes*. They have much the same appearance as potatoes, but their structure is entirely different. When old they become full of brown spores, much like puff balls, but when young they are fleshy in texture. Several species are edible.

These extraordinary underground mushrooms grow round certain types of oak trees known as truffle oaks. Having no stem or root they can only be detected by the faint smell they give off. When fully grown they weigh about 3½ ozs. To unearth these treasures, which is done in winter when they are really ripe and fragrant, the digger needs a mate with a keener sense of smell than himself — a pig or dog.

There are some thirty types of truffle, but the best is the Périgord truffle found around Périgueux, Domme and Sarlat. Production, which reached 1500 tons a century ago, has dropped slightly recently, but new plantations of truffle oaks are being planted, and so production is likely to increase.

In 1986 truffles marketed at the astronomic figure of £288.00 per pound.

WILD MUSHROOMS
The Morel (La Morille)
Unusual among fungi in that they only grow in Spring, morels are found on light soil near trees and hedgerows and grow best on damp warm days. In

appearance they are like knobs of honeycomb on short, stout stalks, but their colour varies between pale yellow and dark grey.

The flavour of this fungus is delicate and aromatic. Fresh or dried they can be used in soups, stews and risottos, as well as being used whole, perhaps stuffed with meat or scrambled egg and lightly fried.

The cep (La Cèpe)
These wonderful edible fungi grow in August and flourish in woodland clearings. For centuries continental housewives have regarded the Cèpe as being the most useful of edible fungi.

In appearance the caps closely resemble old fashioned buns, a smooth dry, polished brown disc 2–6″ across. The underside is a yellowish mass of pores like sponge rubber and the stem is short and fawny-white. The old-wives' tale that colour changes in fungi denote poison is actually true in this case. When picking the Cèpe, break a small piece off the cap. If the flesh remains firm and white you are safe, but if it changes you have gathered a poisonous species. Cèpes can be used in many forms of cooking: soups, rich sauces, in vegetables and as the principal ingredient for Cèpes à la Bordelais: fried in olive oil, then sautéed with butter, garlic and parsley, and served as a starter or a snack.

Morel

Cep

The Epicure's Guide

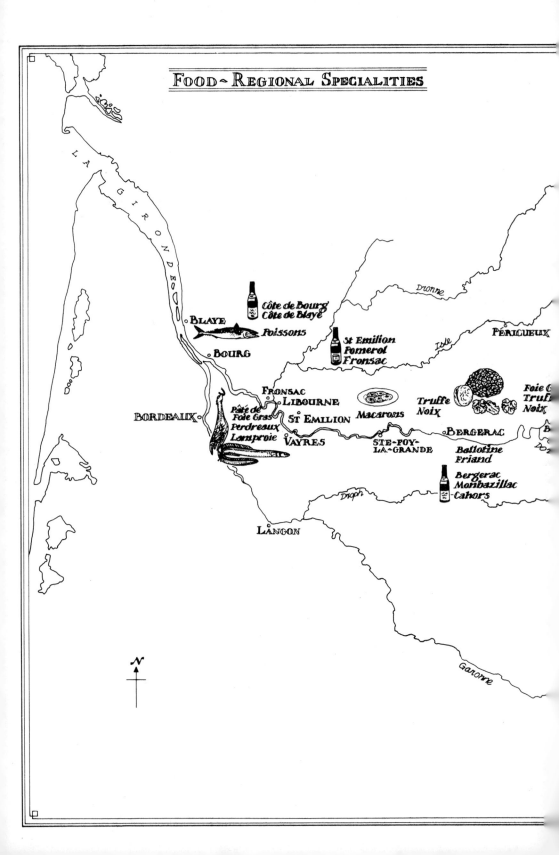

FOOD~REGIONAL SPECIALITIES

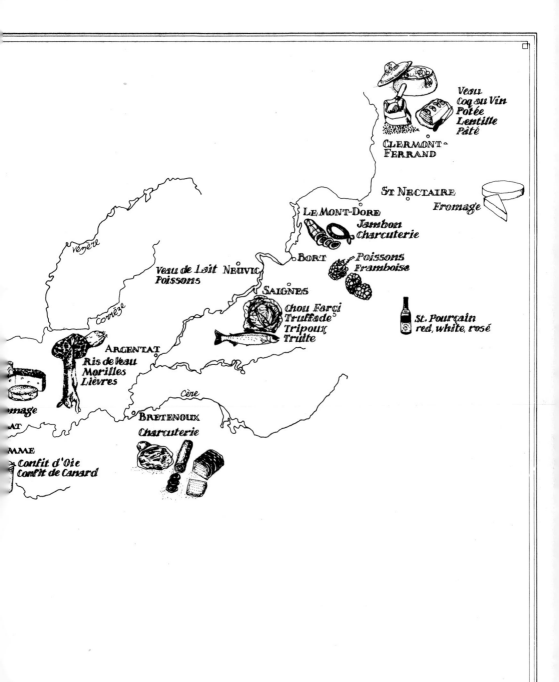

Veau
Coq au Vin
Potée
Lentille
Pâté

CLERMONT-
FERRAND

St NECTAIRE
Fromage

LE MONT-DORE
Jambon
Charcuterie

BORT

Poissons
Framboise

Vézère

Veau de Lait NEUVIC
Poissons

SAIGNES

Chou Farci
Truffade
Tripoux
Truite

St. Pourçain
red, white, rosé

Corrèze

ARGENTAT
Ris de Veau
Morilles
Lièvres

Cère

BRETENOUX
Charcuterie

omage

AT

MME

Confit d'Oie
Confit de Canard

Gastronomy

France is the land of gastronomy, and eating well is one of the pleasures of a holiday there. The cuisine of France is generally acknowledged, especially by the French and francophiles like myself, to be the best and most imaginative in the world. It is the only country in which great chefs are held in the same esteem as opera singers or famous painters, (in England they are lucky if they earn a decent salary, and are often ignored), and where housewives know instinctively the ingredients for a 'daube' or 'pot au feu'.

The French have a completely different attitude towards shopping for the family meal. Instead of rushing once a week to buy everything at the supermarket as often happens in many countries, they spend time going to the best shop or market stall for each ingredient. They choose potatoes with as much care as peaches, and demand just the 'right' cut of meat for the recipe. In the English-speaking world this might be considered an unnecessary performance, but in France it is considered one of the most creative and useful ways of spending one's days.

The same care and attention is taken by French chefs whether in expensive Michelin Rosette restaurants, the family auberge or in the Relais Routiers alongside the road where lorry drivers take their meals. Of course, there are some dull eating establishments in France as in every country. Avoid restaurants/cafés with signs saying 'Bifteck Frites' (Steak and Chips), and loads of tourists outside, and you should have a more interesting time.

There are three, no, two distinctive types of french cuisine — 'haute cuisine' and 'cuisine bourgeoise', for 'la cuisine nouvelle' can hardly be included; who wants to eat raw sweetbreads, steak with strawberries or salads soaked in raspberry vinegar? — ugh!!

The first, 'haute cuisine', has been practised for centuries by a few very distinguished chefs employed originally by royalty or the nobility, and is now only found in very grand establishments at great cost. The second 'cuisine bourgeoise' is, of course, the cooking of the people and the regions. The regional diversity of french cooking is quite amazing. It is true that some dishes are common to most parts of France: but each region also has its own elaborate array of specialities rooted in peasant history and based on local produce, dependent upon soil and climate.

Charcuterie*

Pork features among the many riches of Auvergne — marginally more than in Limousin, for here the climate is just right and air-dried charcuterie is extremely good, indeed you will find Auvergnats selling their charcuterie in markets all over France. In particular look out for 'Andouilles' (small sausages) and 'Friands Sanflourins', little sausages baked in pastry. Their hams are mouthwatering, some baked in pastry with Madeira and 'Boudin' (black pudding). Boudin is often served hot with chestnuts and red cabbage, a hearty meal which is extremely warming in the winter. Pâtés too are good and varied, contrary to those mainly available in England, pork liver predominates and many are highly spiced.

In Périgord and Bordelais charcuterie, common of course throughout France, is typified by the stuffing of meats — especially in Périgord. Here they use the famous foie gras (goose liver) to make galantines (see below) and ballotines (hot galantines), but being made mostly with poultry they cannot strictly be called charcuterie.

Meat, poultry and game

Beef, lamb, mutton, veal, pork, turkeys, geese and chicken are all produced in one part or another of Auvergne and Limousin. Limousin has virtually become the meat factory of France; the Limousin cattle produce first class meat which has changed the local cuisine. Lamb and mutton thrive equally on the well-watered height of the Auvergne. Look out for the famous 'Gigot brayaude'; this delicious dish is almost like a pot roast of leg of lamb cooked on a bed of vegetables and potatoes with a little wine. It should be served with

---

* *La charcuterie*: the pork butcher and delicatessen. The word comes from 'chair cuite', or cooked meat, but uncooked items are also sold. Their shops are fascinating containing not only charcuteries but endless delicacies including bowls of freshly made salads, and tempting home-made local dishes. The ideal shop in which to buy the basis for a wonderful picnic.

Galantine of Chicken

(for 8–10 persons)

1 cooked, boiling chicken
1 lb home-made sausage-meat
4 oz ham cut into 1×3 cm strips
2 hard-boiled eggs peeled and sliced
1½ pints of chicken stock
1 chicken stock cube
6 mushrooms neatly sliced
½ oz pistachio nuts, blanched, skinned and chopped
1 pint of white chaudfroid sauce (Bechamel sauce with aspic, gelatine and cream)

garnish: chopped pimento and strips of lemon rind

Cut down the back of the chicken and remove all the bones carefully and neatly. Flatten out the bird, placing any loose pieces of meat evenly over the surface. Season well. Spread half the sausage-meat on the bird. Arrange the ham, eggs, mushrooms and nuts on top in a symmetrical pattern, season, and cover with the remaining sausage-meat.

Close up the bird, and wrap it up very tightly in foil. Now heat up the stock in a large casserole and add the chicken stock cube, place the chicken parcel into this liquid and simmer for 2½ hours. Allow to cool slightly, remove and drain. Re-tighten the foil around the chicken. Then press the parcel between wooden boards to form an even shape.

When VERY COLD, unwrap, remove the skin and any excess grease, spread with chaudfroid sauce and garnish.

local vegetables — cabbage, red beans and onions. In Auvergne you may find 'sanglier' (boar) casserolled in tons of red wine, and 'Mortier' a casserole of beef or veal with ham and chicken — an unusual combination.

Perhaps the most surprising fact is that 'Coq au Vin' was first cooked here, it was then called 'Coq au Chanturgue'. This is a dish which I am afraid you will not be able to taste in its original form for 'Chanturgue' is one of the wines which has long disappeared as the vineyards have been replaced by pastures.

Périgord has a reputation for extremely fine food. It is a region of 'confits' (poultry preserved in fat), and of every kind of poultry stuffed with swollen livers, chestnuts and truffles. As well as being made into delicious pâté, goose liver is also freshly baked or fried and served hot in a grape and wine sauce. This delicious dish is called 'Foie Gras chaud'.

In Bordelais, along the edge of the Gironde, spring lambs feed on salty grass. There the 'pré-salé' (salt-meadow) lambs develop a flavour which is considered to be unsurpassed. The lamb is normally served roasted with potatoes sautéed with strips of Périgord truffle — a delight to the palate.

The quality of beef and pork is high but there are no distinctive regional recipes worth mentioning.

Other than hare 'lièvre' and partridge there is precious little game nowadays; netting and eating of migrating songbirds (once considered to be a real delicacy) has been forbidden by the laws of the EEC. But if you can find 'Lièvre à la Royale' (a Périgordian speciality), which is boned hare marinated and stuffed with everything expensive (foie gras, truffles) and braised in wine for a very long time, you will be in for a great treat, but at a great price! Partridge 'perdrix' is prepared as a pot roast with cabbage or lentils in the traditional Auvergne way.

La Boucherie — the butcher's shop

The butcher sells beef, pork, veal and lamb. He may sell poultry too and game of course in season. He does not, however, sell horse meat, this is sold in the 'boucherie chevaline' or supermarkets.

In France the midday meal on Sunday is the gastronomic highlight of the week, so the butcher is open on a Sunday morning and closed on Monday. The best thing about French butchers is the quality of their meat whose cuts, unfamiliar to English eyes, are painstakingly prepared, removing every piece of gristle, fat and bone. You will often find that the French themselves buy only their beef, lamb, pork and veal from the butcher, and their poultry direct from a farm. You might pass one advertising 'volailles' . . . but beware, they may expect you to take the thing away squawking!

Fish and shellfish

There is an abundance of fresh water fish in the lakes of Limousin and Auvergne. The most common way in which it will be served in restaurants is as 'friture' which is a fry-up of mixed fresh water fish. Pike 'brochet' is sometimes stuffed or made into pâté, a tastier version of the quenelle. Trout, which is local and wild, is traditionally served in a recipe with cheese and spinach, but personally I think it is better 'au bleu' (poached).

In the 18th century Auvergnat frogs, which I might say are still very tasty, were specifically taken to the Paris market for they were considered to be the most succulent in France. The real treat of this area is the local crayfish 'écrevisses', which are quite delicious cooked just with fresh mint in the Auvergne manner.

Unless you fish yourself you will be most unlikely to sample fish actually from the Dordogne, for it was so overfished in former years that commercial fishing is prohibited. In Périgord there is a marked absence of fish on restaurant menus, and I haven't come across any regional fish recipes in current use.

In Bordelais, as with any area near the sea, many fish are available, but the most typical are shad 'alose', lamphrey 'lamproie' and eels 'anguille'.

Shad is best between April and June and is generally served with sorrel. Lamphrey is a type of eel with an extremely hideous face. They are laborious, to say the least, to prepare, sometimes taking a couple of days, so nowadays few restaurants serve them, and the traditional recipe 'Lamproie à la Bordelais' (thick with leeks and red wine) is fast being forgotten. A quicker version is more likely to be found using ordinary eels.

For the Brit who is getting home-sick by this stage, jellied eels 'anguilles en gelée' can readily be found.

Vegetables and Fruit

In Limousin and Auvergne the most striking use of vegetables is the numerous and delicious potato ideas, for Limousin was one of the very first areas in France to enjoy the potato.

Look out for *Criquettes* — potato pancakes flavoured with garlic; *Farinettes* — savoury pancakes usually filled with potatoes and vegetables and *Aligot* — one of the most famous dishes — a purée of mashed potato and fresh cheese, aligot being the fresh curd of local cheeses.

In Périgord try strawberries soaked in Bergerac wine, and peaches, pears, plums and apricots preserved in local brandy. All are quite delicious if not a little intoxicating. Finally, in Bordelais try artichokes, dipping each tender leaf into a dressing made with the delectable walnut oil.

At the greengrocer (La Fruiterie) you will find that French local-grown vegetables are cheaper and much better than those in England, for the French insist on having fresh vegetables and green salads daily.

Puddings

Best known of the edible sweet delights along the Dordogne is the delicious 'clafoutis' from Limousin. A good old fashioned baked batter pudding containing fresh locally grown cherries.

The cake shop (La Patisserie) is a den of iniquity. If you are worried about the waistline then hurry past their extremely tempting window displays. The French go in for pastry, not cakes as we know them. They are altogether much lighter, full of fruit and often oozing with cream.

Clafoutis

Clafoutis

4 whole eggs
7 oz flour
a pinch of salt
1 pint of milk
2 tablespoons of oil
5½ oz sugar
14 oz fresh dark red unpitted cherries
1/5 pint rum

Put the flour and salt into a mixing bowl. Add ½ the milk, oil and the eggs and beat with a wooden spoon. Pour in the rest of the milk, the rum, and a ⅓ of the sugar and mix to a smooth batter. Leave aside for 1 hour.

Butter a deep baking tin and line it with the cherries. Pour over the batter and place a few knobs of butter over the surface. Bake in a hot oven at 410° F. for 30-35 mins. When cooked sprinkle with the remaining sugar.

Cheese

France is a country of cheeses, there are over 400 cheeses listed in France and many more that are not recorded. Every region and many villages have their own speciality, and the cheeses that you will experience along the Dordogne are equal to none.

Aligot (Rouergue). Originating in the mountains of Aubrac, aligot is a fresh pressed cheese that has to be eaten within 48 hours of manufacture. Produced by small mountain dairies called burons it is slightly sour with a somewhat nutty flavour; used in cooking.

Bleu d'Auvergne A.O.C.* Only created in 1845 by a peasant of the Auvergne who added some of the blue mould he saw on his rye bread to his cheeses and

* Apellation d'origine contrôllée: an award given to certain cheese and other highly outstanding foods by the same body that awards the A.O.C. to wine. Other products include: lentils from Le Puy, chickens from Bresse and walnuts from Grenoble.

poked them with a needle to ensure the air passages needed for the mould to grow. Others in the area followed his example and so was born one of the newest cheeses to be honoured with an A.O.C.

Cantalon. Produced in most of Auvergne, it is a cow's milk cheese similar to cantal.

Fourme d'Ambert or Fourme de Montbrison A.O.C. The cheese we know probably emerged in the 8th or 9th century, although it has a history that pre-dates the arrival of the Caesars. Fourme refers to moulds in which the cheese is made. It is a typical blue pressed uncooked cow's milk cheese but has a rougher, more mould-covered crust than most. Produced extensively in the farms and dairies of the Puy-de-Dôme plus some in the neighbouring Loire (Rhone Valley) and five cantons around St. Flour. It has a smooth fruity flavour.

St. Nectaire A.O.C. An outstanding cheese of great antiquity. It is a pressed cow's milk cheese, made in farms and dairies in a large area of south-west Puy-de-Dôme and the north of Cantal. The crust is brine-washed during curing to encourage moulds varying in colour from white to red and violet. Best eaten in summer and autumn; frequently used in cooking.

Couhe-Verac. Soft goat's milk cheese, wrapped in plane tree or chestnut leaves. Best from late spring to early autumn. Named after nearest town to its farm-based production.

Echourgnac. Made in the monastery of Echourgnac in the Périgord. Small washed-rind cheese with tiny holes in the body.

Rocamadour. Known also as cabecou de Rocamadour, made from sheep's milk in the spring and goat's milk in the summer. A tiny disc of cheese that when aged with wine or spirit in crocks is known as a picadou.

La Fromagerie — the cheese shop
Devoted entirely to cheese. Often you will be able to taste the varieties before buying. (Note: cheese is taken before dessert in France.)

Wine

'France is the undisputed mistress of the vine; the producer of infinitely more and more varied great wines than all the rest of the world.'

Hugh Johnson

Wine, like bread, is one of the basics of life and makes the perfect accompaniment to food.

The best way to widen your knowledge of wine is to drink it, but a few hints will help you get the best value for your money. When travelling through France, the local wine is normally the best value and by far the most fun to try. Don't go for the cheapest 'Vin Ordinaire', unless you plan to drink the white with Cassis (blackcurrant liqueur) as a Kir, but go for the region's Vins de Pays or V.D.Q.S. appellation, this way you will avoid disappointment.

There are three main places to buy wine in France; at the Grocer or supermarket, at a specialist wine shop, or at a vineyard or co-operative. The first is of course very convenient, the second will probably offer sound advice, but the third is the most fun.

Almost every wine-growing commune in France has a Cave Co-opérative or at least several vineyards who welcome passers-by. It is very easy to find these, for they will have the word 'Dégustation' (tastings) displayed on the road and sometimes 'Dégustation Gratuite' (free tastings), even better. The former does not mean that you pay to taste the wine, but it means that it is a courtesy to buy a bottle or two when you leave. If you visit several vineyards on your travels, you will not only accumulate a few bottles for your country picnics, but some good presents to take home.

The only other point worth mentioning, before I give you a quick résumé of the districts that you will visit along the Dordogne, is that some 'Caves' are closed during August, so why not travel in late September, enjoy many dégustations and watch the harvest in the full glory of the Autumn sun.

The Massif Central

The wines from the départements of Allier and Puy-de-Dôme are in fact classified as Loire wines, but in style the delightful wines of *St. Pourçain* have more in common with those of Burgundy. The whites are crisp and flowery, the reds and rosés fruity. The *Côtes d'Auvergne* wines are very agreeable, the reds resembling fruity Beaujolais.

Dordogne and the Lot

The two best known wines from this area are *Bergerac* and *Cahors*. The red of Cahors, can be drunk young, whilst the finest cuvées are kept for at least three years in oak casks and become the appellation *Vieux Cahors*. These wines are rustic and full-bodied.

The wines from Bergerac are softer and the appellation covers both reds and rosés. The excellent dry whites, appellation *Bergerac Sec*, are crisp and clean, the reds are full of fruit and charm, and the rarer *Pécharment*, the best red wine from the Dordogne, is at its best after 3–6 years. *Monbazillac* is the best of the white wines within Bergerac. It is honey-sweet and once rivalled the great *Sauternes*. Finally there are the Vins de Pays, of which the fruity and refreshing *Vin de Glanes* is probably the best.

Aquitaine

St. Emilion makes a rich red wine which on the whole takes less long than those of the Médoc to reach perfection. There are two distinct districts of St. Emilion. The first borders onto *Pomerol*: the most famous château on this plateau is *Château Cheval Blanc*, a small white-washed house, whose appearance belies its splendid and famous wine. The second, is the *Côtes St. Emilion* which occupies the escarpment around the town. The most famous château here is *Château Ausone*, which produces excellent wines, but perhaps slightly less fruity than those from the plateau. If budget is a problem, and believe me it can be in St. Emilion, then visit the lesser known château; *Montagne-Saint Emilion*, for example, produces excellent wines at very reasonable prices.

The Romans had vineyards in Pomerol, yet even 30 years ago it was hardly recognised. Today it is noted for expensive wines of the highest quality. There is no real village in Pomerol, every family makes wine. The landscape is evenly dotted with modest houses, known as wine châteaux, and a church stands isolated on the horizon. Pomerol is a gentle, rich and most appealing claret

KEY TO WINE REGIONS

1 Médoc
2 Graves
3 Premières Côtes de Bordeaux
4 Loupiac
5 St. Croix~du~Mont
6 Bordeaux St. Macaire
7 Graves de Vayres
8 Entre~Deux~Mers
9 St. Foy Bordeaux

10 Blayais
11 Bourgeais
12 Charente Maritime
13 Fronsac
14 Pomerol
15 Lalande~de~Pomerol
16 St. Emilion
17 St. Emilion (others)
18 Bordeaux Côtes de Francs
19 Castillon

20 Bergerac
21 Montravel
22 Rosette
23 Pécharment
24 Monbazillac
25 Côtes de Saussignac
26 Côtes de Duras

with a deep colour. The area has a reputation for reliability so you will enjoy almost anything you buy.

Château Petrus is certainly one of the best Pomerols, and is definitely the most well-known and highly priced. Though whether this is due to its intrinsic excellence or the unstinting publicity efforts of its owner, Madame Loubat, who died in 1961, seems open to discussion. All the wine is bottled on the estate and has a very full and rich taste.

Situated about a mile from Libourne is *Fronsac*. As a whole Fronsac is reputed to be the coming thing in Bordeaux. These red wines are for laying down, they are splendidly fruity and full of character, and are also still quite cheap.

Bourg and *Blaye* are productive little districts producing the sort of wine that everyone wants, reliable, enjoyable and cheap. The Bourg district offers principally red wines which are round and fruity, try *Château du Bousquet* and *Château Mille Secousses*. In Blaye the emphasis is on the production of moderate dry white wines which are extremely palatable, try *Château Monconseil.*

Excellent years for St. Emilion and Pomerol are: 1961, 1966, 1970, 1971, 1975, 1976, 1982, 1983 and 1985.

The classes of wine

1. Appellations d'Origine Contrôlées — A.O.C. Guaranteed not only of origin but of a certain standard, administered by the Central 'Institut National des Appellations d'Origine' in Paris.
2. V.D.Q.S. — Vin Délimité de Qualité Supérieure. Good wines of chiefly local interest.
3. Vins de Pays — introduced in 1973 to give recognition to the more modest wine producer previously disregarded, but whose output is well worth investigation.
4. Co-operatives — A central wine-making factory, owned by the farmers (with bank backing) where they produce their wines efficiently and economically.

Handy Tips

HOW TO GET THERE FROM THE UK
By Air Airports at Bordeaux, Limoges and Clermont-Ferrand. Daily direct flights Heathrow–Bordeaux by British Airways/Air France. Car hire facilities are available at each airport, prebooking advisable. Heathrow–Bordeaux have Fly/Drive package options.

By Rail Victoria Station, London to Clermont-Ferrand via Paris, then local train to Saignes. Travel time 12–13 hours approximately, car hire should be pre-booked.

By Car Ferry crossings Dover to Boulogne or Calais are the cheapest and quickest (1½ hours). Take the Autoroutes to Paris, and then go south via Bourges or Nevers. Alternatively, to avoid Paris, take the western route via Rouen and Orléans to Bourges. This route has little autoroute driving. Ferries to Le Havre take 4–5 hours, cost more but entail less driving, take the autoroute to Rouen and then south to Orléans and Bourges.

Although it is possible to drive to Dordogne in one day, it is more usual and comfortable to allow for an overnight stop — perhaps on the Loire at Orléans or Gien.

By Bus Regular service to Bordeaux from Victoria Station, London. Peak summer season has daily departures, journey time 24 hours.

WHEN TO GO
Any time from Easter to the end of September. In a good Autumn, warm sunny weather will last to the end of October.

Try to avoid travelling on or just before or after a bank holiday (see below). The worst time for traffic is the first weekend in August, when nearly every French family is on the move.

HOTELS
It is advisable to book hotels in advance especially between July and

September. Most hotels along the river Dordogne close from the end of October until the beginning of March.

FISHING
Rivers are divided into two categories. In La Première Catégorie trout and salmon predominate, and maggots are banned; in La Deuxième catégorie, almost anything can be caught with the exception of fish eggs. Angling shops will advise on the correct licence for the area (le permis de pêche).

CAMPING AND CARAVANNING
There are some wonderful sites along the whole length of the Dordogne. Buy the green Michelin Camping and Caravanning guide for addresses. Unlike dreary England even the smallest of sites has electricity. N.B. Don't forget your Caravan Club of Great Britain registration carnet.

DRIVING
Driving on the right is usually no problem, the danger only comes when returning to the road from a car park, a petrol station and of course at roundabouts. Until recently priority was always given to those approaching from the right. This custom is fast changing and roundabouts can therefore be treated in the English style, but beware drivers turning from small roads in towns and country lanes. Traffic police can be tough even on foreign motorists who are caught speeding, overshooting a red light or failing to wear seat belts, so take care. Seat belts are obligatory everywhere in France outside town limits.

ROAD NUMBERS
The French government, which used to be responsible for numbering all the roads in France, has started to hand over this responsibility to the individual départements. In their wisdom the individual départements have in some cases decided to renumber the roads and as you can imagine this process is not only slow but confusing. I have tried to be as correct as possible with the road numbers, but you may unfortunately find some discrepancies. For example you could come across a road marked as the N137 when it is really the D 937.

SPEED LIMITS
Autoroutes	130 kmph (80 mph)
Dual Carriageways	110 kmph (68 mph)

Other Roads	90 kmph (56 mph)
Built-up areas	60 kmph (37 mph), or as directed by signs

Autoroutes nearly all have periodic tolls (péages) and can be expensive on long journeys.

THE METRIC SYSTEM

Kilometres — for road distances 8 km equals 5 miles thus:

Km:miles	Km:miles	Km:miles
3:2	10:6	80:50
4:2½	20:12	90:56
5:3	30:18	100:62
6:3½	40:25	125:78
7:4	50:31	150:94
8:5	60:37	175:110
9:5½	70:44	200:125

Litres — the British (imperial) gallon is just over 4½ litres, the US gallon about 3¾ litres, thus:

Litres	Brit Gal	US Gal
5	1.1	1.3
10	2.2	2.7
15	3.3	4.0
20	4.4	5.3
30	6.7	8.0
40	8.8	10.6
50	11.1	13.3
100	22.2	26.7

When you get used to the price of motor fuel (essence) in France you may find it simplest to order it in multiples of 10 francs. Petrol is marginally more expensive in France than the UK. The easiest way to overcome language problems in this area is simply to say 'plein' which is 'full'.

Tyre Pressure — measured in Kilograms per square centimetre. To convert lbs/sq. in. to Kg/sq cm, divide by 100 and multiply by 7. Thus:

lbs/sq in	Kg/sq cm
18	1.25
20	1.4
22	1.55
24	1.7

lbs/sq in	Kg/sq cm
26	1.8
28	2.0
30	2.1
32	2.25
34	2.4

BANK HOLIDAYS
Nothing is more annoying than to land in France with no currency, to find that it is a bank holiday and the banks and shops are shut.

New Year's Day	1st January
Easter Monday	Variable
Labour Day	1st May
V.E. Day	8th May
Ascension Day	6th Thursday after Easter
Whit Monday	2nd Monday after Ascension
Bastille Day	14th July
Assumption	15th August
All Saints (Toussaint)	1st November
Armistice Day	11th November
Christmas Day	25th December

BANKS
Banks are shut on Saturdays and Sundays, except in towns with a Saturday market, when they open on Saturday and shut on Monday. Banks also close at midday on the eve of bank holidays.

Banking hours are normally 8 a.m.–12 noon and 2–4.30 p.m. When changing cheques or travellers cheques remember your passport and Eurocheque encashment card or other internationally recognised cheque card.

TELEPHONING
It is cheapest to use the modern coin boxes. Slots take 5 francs, 1 franc and ½ franc pieces. You can put plenty of money in before you start as it is returned if unused.

Calls within the same département: dial the 6-figure number.
Calls to another département: *dial 16*, listen for the tone change, then dial the area code (*2 figures*), followed by the 6 figure number.
Calls to the U.K.: *dial 19*, listen for tone change, then *dial 44*, followed by U.K.

code (omitting the '0') and then the number you want.
Calls to other European countries: consult directory.
Transatlantic: consult hotel or post office.

All French area codes are listed at the beginning of telephone directories.

SHOP OPENING TIMES
These vary according to a) season b) type of shop c) size of town. In most places shops are open on Saturday, but may be shut on Monday. Food shops (baker, butcher, general store) tend to shut later than others, sometimes as late as 7 p.m., some open on Sundays and bank holiday mornings. Generally all shops close for 2–3 hours at lunchtime from midday.

RAILWAYS
S.N.C.F. — Société Nationale de Chemin de Fer. The trains are generally very clean, comfortable and punctual. It is best to buy tickets in advance from mainline stations or travel agents. Seats can be reserved on main lines. Hire cars can be booked in advance in most large towns. Bicycles can be hired at stations.

Men over 65 and women over 60, on production of their passport, can obtain a 'carte vermeil' entitling them to a 50% reduction on non-rush hour trains.

Note: Many stations have automatic punch ticket machines (red machine) on the platform, this dates your ticket. If you do not get your ticket punched by one of these machines you can be charged again, plus a fine of 20%, so be careful.

SPEAKING FRENCH
Outside the major tourist attractions, it is safer not to rely on finding English spoken much and so it is helpful and courteous to take a two-way phrase book and a dictionary.

TIPPING
Most restaurants and hotels automatically add 15% service, if they don't 15% is expected. Bell boys and tour guides also expect tips.

MONUMENTS AND MUSEUMS
Opening times and prices of admission have not been included in this book,

as they are subject to change. All places mentioned are open to the public and will charge a few francs admission. Normally they will be open from Easter to the end of October, from 9.30–12.00 a.m. and from 3–5 p.m.

Note: Guided tours will cease admission half an hour before closing.

KEY TO ITINERARY

Ratings are for prices/room/night.

★★   Reasonable
★★★   Average
★★★★   Expensive
★★★★★   Very expensive

Names of the hotels and restaurants which are the first choice of the author are printed in **bold** and are distinguished by the following symbols:

Lunch   Dinner

The Itinerary

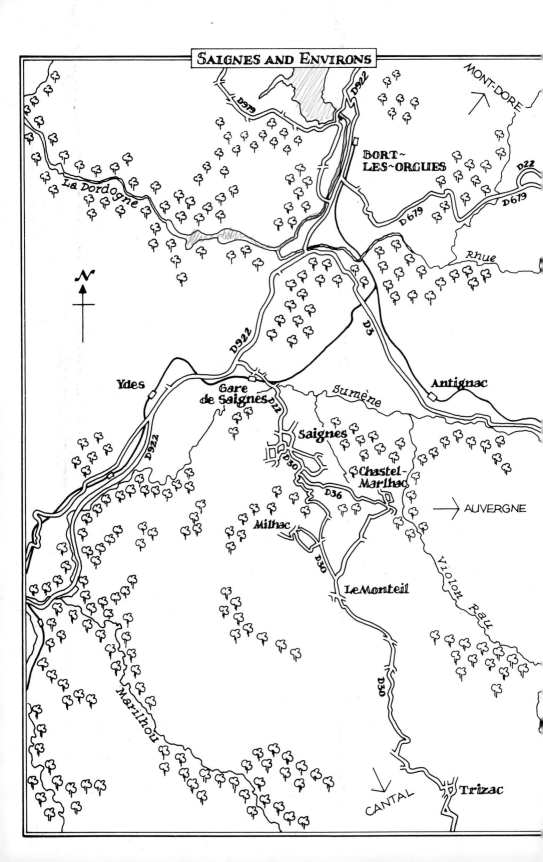

The Journey Begins

DAY 1

Arrive at Saignes, discover this little village on foot and walk up the steep mound to the 12th century Chapel of Notre Dame.

Saignes (pronounced Sagnes) is a sleepy unspoilt village situated on the borders of Auvergne and Limousin. The village was originally surrounded by marshland, but due to agricultural improvements over the ages, and its mild climate, the land has been transformed into fertile fields and grazing land creating the parish of Saignes as it is today; a charming oasis encircled by basaltic and volcanic rock.

In the main square stands the 12th century Norman church, l'Eglise de St. Croix, which was restored in about 1900.

Just off this square in a little side street is the Town Hall which was built in 1895. The original Town Hall was erected in 1573 under the rule of the 'Chabannes', this cannot be seen today as it was demolished in 1884, but once served as a covered market, the law courts, and a place for village meetings.

Behind the square perched on the top of an impressive rock stands the ruined keep of an 11th century castle, destroyed by the English in 1387, and the picturesque 12th century Chapel of Notre Dame.

From this mound there is a magnificent view of the rich green fields, the plateaus of Chastel-Marlhac and Milhac, and on the horizon the mountain chains of Dore and Cantal which are relics of the ancient volcanos of Auvergne.

Dinner and overnight at **Le Relais Arverne**.

Le Relais Arverne
15240 Saignes
Tel: (71) 40 62 64

A most attractive turreted building in the corner of the lovely rural square of this little village. From the front bedrooms one can see the 12th century Chapel of Notre Dame perched on top of an impressive volcanic peak, and from the back bedrooms there are views over the valley.

The hotel is owned by M. et Mme. Cosnefroy. Alain Cosnefroy is an excellent chef who will quite willingly show you his spotless kitchen: indeed, the whole hotel is very clean. The dining room is traditionally French, and the rooms, although some are small, are furnished with care.

Warm and friendly atmosphere.

Closed:	15th January to 15th February
Rooms:	11
Facilities:	Bar, Restaurant, Conference Room, car park.
Credit cards:	Visa, Eurocard (Access, Mastercard)
Food:	Try Pot au Feu de la Mer au Beurre Rouge (refer to p. 133 for other specialities).
Wine:	Try St. Pourçain and Framboise liqueur.
Rating:	★★

LES TERRASSES
15240 **Saignes**
Tel: (71) 40 63 75

Again in the square. A smaller establishment with a pretty terrace, hence the name.

Friendly with a good fixed price menu.

Closed:	15th December to 31st January
Rooms:	10
Facilities:	Bar, Dining Room
Credit cards:	Eurocard (Access, Mastercard)
Food:	Menu changes regularly
Wine:	Good, honest house wine
Rating:	★★

SAIGNES: USEFUL INFORMATION

Tourist Office:	small office near Town Hall
Population:	960
Altitude:	480 metres
Sports:	heated swimming pool
	2 tennis courts
	French bowls (Pétanque)
	archery
Facilities:	station about 1 mile from village
	2 camping sites
	Huttes de France (chalets for hire)
	hotels
Festivals:	
June:	Fête de la Saint Jean
1st Sunday July:	Fête de l'Age d'ôr
3rd Sunday July:	Kermesse Paroissiale
1st Sunday August:	Fête des Cités d'Automne
3rd Sunday August:	Foire à la Brocante de Valée de la Sumène

Saignes

DAY 2

Based at Saignes today's trip will take you up to the mountains of Auvergne for lunch, via the post war Barrage de Bort, and in contrast the fairytale 15th century Château de Val, which was once perched high above the river like an eagle's eyrie.

Total mileage: 74 miles

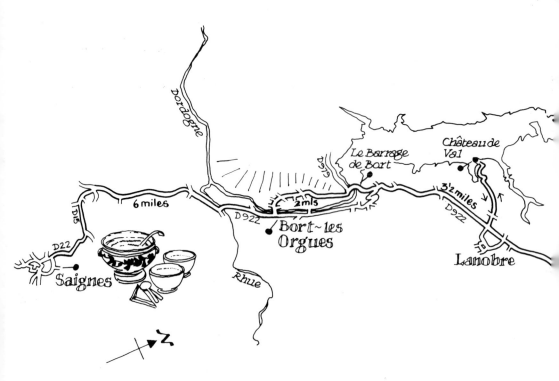

Leave Saignes for day.

After breakfast at Le Relais Arverne take the D22/D15/D922 to Bort-les-Orgues.

Bort-les-Orgues.

This ancient town on the banks of the Dordogne was named after the immense rocks which tower 1050 ft above it. Originally formed by outflows of volcanic rock, they have been moulded by time to resemble large organ pipes.

Walk up the little street past the covered market and the Town Hall to Place Jeanne d'Arc. Look around the 12th century church and note its striking modern stained glass windows. These were made by Jacques Bourchie in 1973.

After stopping in one of the numerous cafés by the river for coffee, take the D979 to Le Barrage de Bort.

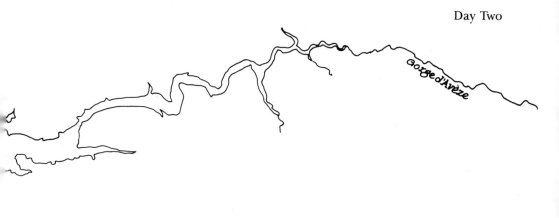

Le Barrage de Bort

This remarkable structure is a gravity arch dam. Built about 1950, it is 360 ft high, 1070 ft across, 240 ft thick at the base, and 24 ft at the top. The reservoir behind it holds 477 million cubic metres of water, making it the 2nd largest in France.

From here take the D922 signposted to Tauves and just before the village of Lanobre turn left down a little winding lane to Le Château de Val.

Le Château de Val

This château stands majestically on a rocky islet, its fine outlines lapped by the waters of the vast Lac de Bort. It was built in the 15th century and is flanked by 6 towers with pepper pot roofs. The chapel beside it is gothic and is dedicated to St. Plaise. The château contains some admirable fireplaces with multi-coloured carvings, decorated ceilings and marquetry floors, and from the parapet walk there is a magnificent view over the lake. The château is open to the public.

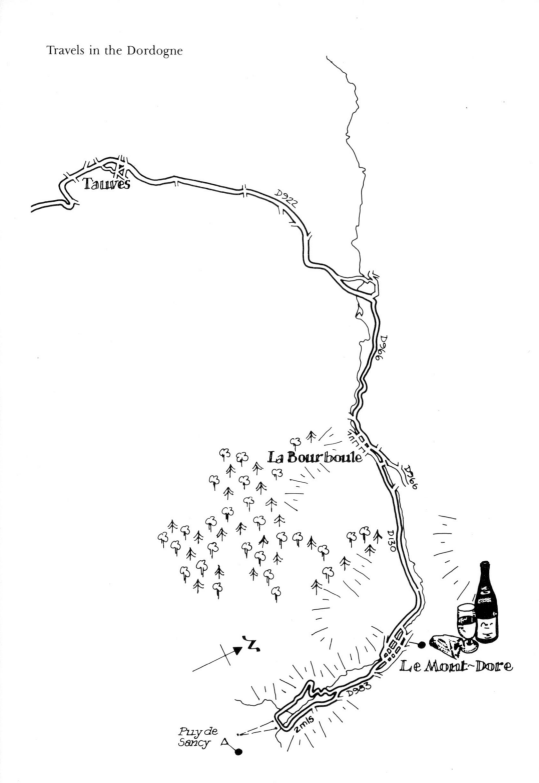

There is a regular ferry trip around the lake which is well worth the time (approximately 30 minutes).

Return to the D922 and follow on to the D966 through La Bourboule then the D130 to Le Mont-Dore.

Le Mont-Dore

Nestling in a beautiful wooded valley of beeches and firs in the very heart of Auvergne, lies Le Mont-Dore (Puy-de-Dôme). This town has been universally recognised since Roman times as a great spa for respiratory complaints and no less than eight hot springs rise in the thermal baths.

There are numerous restaurants, I recommend in particular **La Belle Epôque**. Lunch should be simple, try la soupe aux chou, a plate of local charcuterie and St. Nectaire, a cheese made close by which was once served to the Kings of France.

After lunch drive out on the D983 to the cable car.

Puy de Sancy 1780 metres

The valley at the source of the Dordogne is dominated by the Massif du Sancy, the highest point in central France. It is essential to take the cable car to the top of Puy de Sancy, from where one can walk through breathtaking scenery and admire the panorama. If you are feeling energetic it is possible to take the cable car up and walk all the way down.

Leave Sancy and drive back towards Le Mont-Dore — stop beside the Dordogne and walk.

At the foot of Sancy where the river Dore and the river Dogne meet is the place where the Dordogne rises, swift flowing and speckled with foam it starts its 310 mile journey to the estuary near Bordeaux.

Return to Saignes.

Dinner and overnight at **Le Relais Arverne.**

La Belle Epôque
1 Rue Sauvagnat
63240 **Le Mont-Dore**
Tel: (73) 65 07 68

An attractive little restaurant specialising in Auvergne food and wine with a very good chef — Michel Tressy.

Try, La Soupe au Chou, Clafoutis and St. Nectaire.

LE MONT-DORE: USEFUL INFORMATION

Tourist Office:	Avenue Gen. Leclerc
	63240 Le Mont-Dore
	Auvergne
	Tel: (73) 65 20 21
Population:	2400
Altitude:	1050 metres
Sports:	golf (9 holes) — a most beautiful mountain course
	mini golf — in town
	pigeon shooting
	riding
	tennis — 4 all weather courts
	fishing — 5 miles away is the well stocked Lac de Guery
	bowling alley
	2 french bowls (Pétanque)

From December to Easter, Le Mont-Dore is a winter resort with 20 ski lifts, 22 miles of track, cross country skiing and ice skating.

Evening entertainment:	casino with dancing
	2 cinemas
	4 night clubs
Facilities:	hotels
	3 camping sites
	station

Facilities (contd.)	thermal springs health resort
Festivals:	throughout the summer there are numerous folklore, arts and sports meetings

HOTEL CENTRAL
65 Avenue Gare
19110 **Bort-les-Orgues**
Comeze
Tel: (55) 96 74 82

The entrance is from the main road, but there is a large terrace overlooking the river, town and the tremendous rocks from which this town got its name. Ideal for coffee and pastries before your journey to Le Mont-Dore.

Closed:	10th January to 1st March
Rooms:	25
Facilities:	Terrace bar and Dining Room
Credit cards:	Visa, Eurocard
Rating:	★★★

BORT-LES-ORGUES: USEFUL INFORMATION

Tourist Office:	Office de Tourisme Place Marmontel Tel: (55) 96 02 49
Population:	6000
Altitude:	430 metres
Sports:	heated swimming pool tennis court stadium fishing and sailing in the Lac de Bort
Facilities:	station SNCF 3 camping sites hotels

The Great Dams

DAY 3

From Saignes to Argentat.

Today you will leave Saignes and drive downstream through the province of Limousin to the picturesque riverside town of Argentat. From the 'Site de St. Nazaire' on top of the Limousin Plateaux you will see the river pass through a spectacular, deep, wooded valley. The river then flows on through a succession of large lakes and dams until it winds peacefully down to Argentat. Lunch will be taken in the **Restaurant Bellevue** in Neuvic which nestles in the hillside.

Total mileage: 55.5 miles.

Leave Saignes

After breakfast at Le Relais Arverne take the D22/D15/D922/D979 to Le Barrage de Bort.

Between Bort-les-Orgues and Argentat where the river used to flow between narrow ravines, there are now a series of reservoirs and dams forming a gigantic water stairway.

Le Barrage de Bort

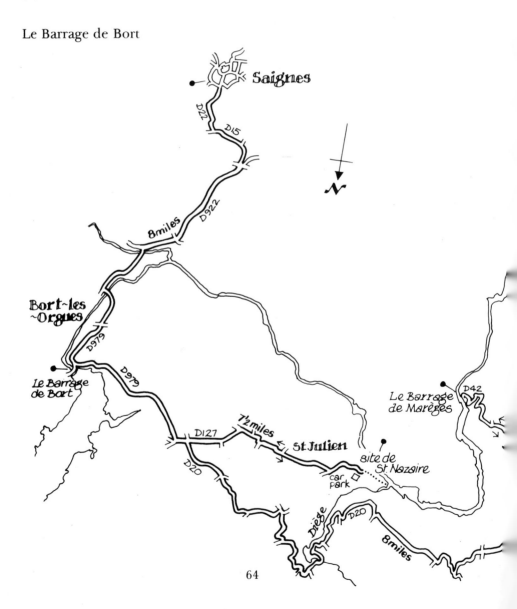

Pass over Le Barrage de Bort and on the right you will find a belvedere from where there is a magnificent view of the Lac de Bort and its fairylike Château de Val.

Site de St. Nazaire

Take the D979/D20/D127 to St. Julien, turn left to the Site de St. Nazaire, park the car and walk along the ridge. The village and church of St. Nazaire once stood at the end of this promontary, which stands high above the point where the rivers Diège and Dordogne come together.

Today all that remains is a calvary and a statue of the Saint on a stone Pyramid. Pilgrimages here started again in 1894, and continue sporadically.

Belvedere

Return to St. Julien turn back onto D127 and left onto D20, a small detour off this road to the left will take you to another belvedere from where one can clearly see the rivers Diège and Dordogne converging amongst the most magnificent scenery.

Le Barrage de Marèges

Drive on to Le Barrage de Marèges, by way of the D20/left to D42E/D42. The road here crosses the Diège and descends to the dam by a series of steep bends.

Completed in 1935, Le Barrage de Marèges is the second of four dams which make up the hydroelectric systems on the Dordogne. The power station of this arched dam, 295 ft high, has a capacity of 340 million kwh and supplies some of the electricity to the French railway system.

Turn around and take the D42/D20 to

Le Barrage Neuvic d'Ussel

This dam, again of the arched type, is 89 ft high and 470 ft long and controls the waters of the Triouzoune, a tributary flowing into the Dordogne from the north.

After this dam, a road runs off to Neuvic beach on the lake behind the dam — where there is a sailing school and a centre for water skiing.

Neuvic

Cross over this dam and continue on to the attractive village of Neuvic which nestles in the hillside amid green surroundings. There is a very interesting museum to visit here, La Musée de la Résistance (also called the Musée André Queuille), where the collection of old photographs and clothes brings the drama of the local resistance fighters strongly to life. The narrow cobbled streets are very pretty, complete with shutters and turrets.

Lunch at **Hotel Bellevue**, Neuvic.

Pont de St. Projet

After lunch take the D982 towards L'Aigle to the graceful suspension bridge — Le Pont de St. Projet — which crosses over the L'Aigle reservoir.

Continue on the D982 which follows the narrow, wooded Labiou valley. Take the D682 on the right and then turn right again onto the D105 to Le Barrage de L'Aigle.

Le Barrage de L'Aigle

Le Barrage de L'Aigle completed in 1947 is the third of the four main dams on the upper Dordogne. The Barrage is impressive for both its size and its bold concept: it has two ski-jump flood control gates in the centre. With a height of 312 ft, 952 ft along the crest, 156 ft thick at the base, the power station produces 460 million kwh annually.

Take the D105 through the tiny village of Aynes which was built in slate and stone for the people concerned in the construction of the dam, and bear right onto the D978 which runs alongside the reservoir of Le Barrage du Chastang as far as Spontour.

There is no road running beside the river now, so a detour along the D978/ D18/D29 has to be made before you rejoin the Dordogne at Le Barrage du Chastang.

Travels in the Dordogne

Le Barrage du Chastang

Le Barrage du Chastang, the fourth and last of the great dams on the upper Dordogne, produces the most electricity of all the dams along the river.

About one mile from the dam on the D29 a narrow path leads down to a belvedere from where the view of the dam and its reservoir is superb.

Servières Le Château

Further along the D29 is Servières Le Château. The castle was set on fire in 1916 by the German officers who were interned there. It has since been rebuilt as a nursing home, affording beautiful views over the deep gorges of the Glane.

Return to the dam and take the D129 along the left bank of the river past Le Gibanel castle across the water to Argentat.

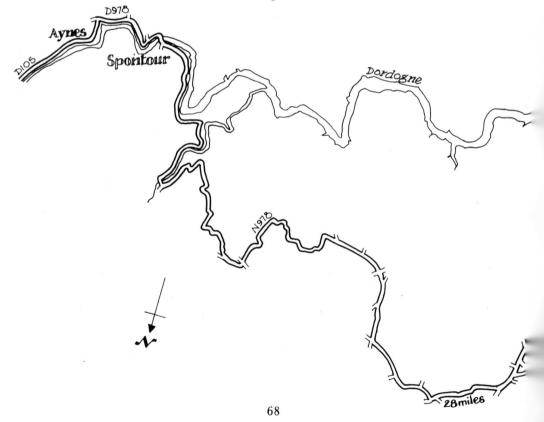

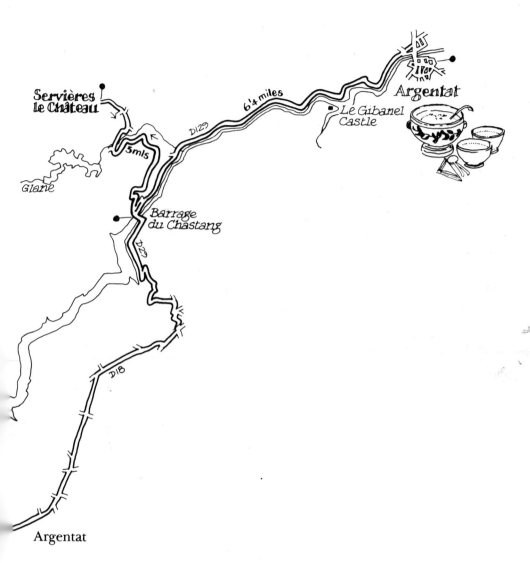

Argentat

Argentat is a pretty town where the old tiled houses with wooden balconies, and the two church spires, reflect perfectly in the river beside the old quay. There are numerous little streets through which to meander slowly. In a small square tucked behind the shorter, square-towered church is the birthplace and monument to General Antoine Guillaume Delmas, who died in battle at Leipzig in 1813 after serving France for 25 years.

Dinner and overnight at **Hotel Gilbert**, Argentat.

Hotel Bellevue
Restaurant
Neuvic
Tel: (55) 95 80 61

This charming restaurant is tucked away behind the square in a quaint narrow cobbled street (well-signposted).

The dining room is beamed and always full of fresh foliage and flowers, a very refreshing sight after the green forested gorges of the Dordogne River.

Excellent restaurant catering mainly for locals (always a good sign). Try local charcuterie and cheese washed down with a pichet of house wine.

The proprietors and staff will give you a warm welcome.

Credit cards: Visa

ESCARGOT
Neuvic
Tel: (55) 95 80 19

A small friendly establishment, good value menu, again favoured by the locals.

Credit cards: Visa

NEUVIC: USEFUL INFORMATION	
Tourist Office:	Tours des Remparts
	(open mornings only)
	Tel: (55) 95 88 78
Population:	2306
Altitude:	610 metres
Sports:	golf
	water sports at Neuvic Plage
	sailing school
	fishing
	tennis
Facilities:	hotel
	camping site
Market day:	Tuesday

Hotel Gilbert
Rue Vachal
19400 **Argentat**
Tel: (55) 28 01 62

The Hotel Gilbert is a good, clean and nicely furnished hotel in the centre of Argentat, within walking distance of all the sights. Here you can spend a comfortable night and enjoy a well cooked dinner.

Closed:	20th December to 1st February
Rooms:	30
Facilities:	Bar, Restaurant, garden and car park
Credit cards:	American Express, Diners Club, Visa
Food:	A varied good quality menu
Wine:	Try Vin de Cahors
Rating:	★★★

HOTEL FOUILLADE
Place Gambetta
19400 **Argentat**
Tel: (55) 28 10 17

This hotel is centrally situated and comfortable, and offers good food at very reasonable prices.

Closed:	4th November to 10th December
Rooms:	30
Facilities:	Bar, Restaurant, garden and car park
Credit cards:	None
Rating:	★★

ARGENTAT: USEFUL INFORMATION

Tourist Office:	Open 15th June to 15th September Tel: (55) 28 10 91
Population:	3725
Altitude:	188 metres
Sports:	swimming pool tennis fishing canoeing
Facilities:	hotels, camp sites, station

Les Cascades de Murel

DAY 4

From Argentat to Goulles

Waterfalls, Norman churches, and the feudal fortress 'Le Tours de Merle' with its impressive son et lumière, make up today's excursion, together with a light lunch, and a traditional french dinner at **Le Relais du Teulet —** Goulles.

Total mileage: 41.5 miles

Leave Argentat

After breakfast at the Hotel Gilbert leave Argentat by the N120 to Tulle and then left on D113/D113E to the Cascade de Murel, in the valley of the Souvigne.

Cascade de Murel

These beautiful waterfalls, a short distance on foot from the car park, are situated amongst picturesque wooded glades.

Albussac

Take the D113/D87 to the hamlet of Albussac. In the centre of this rather uninteresting hamlet stands a very beautiful 12th century church with a pre-Norman choir.

Drive on towards Neuville and cross over the N121, taking the D169 back to Argentat.

Argentat

Take the D980 to St. Privat, turn right onto the D13 to St. Cirgues La Loutre for a light lunch on the terrace of the **Auberge des Ruines de Merle.**

St. Cirgues La Loutre

After lunch have a look at the charming 13th century church and then proceed to the ancient citadel of Merle — 'Tours de Merle'.

These ruins which stand sedately above the waters of the Maronne are all that remain of the feudal fortress 'Le Tours de Merle'.

In the Middle Ages the Lords of Merle were the most feared in the region and their domain was considered to be impregnable, even the English failed to conquer it during the Hundred Years' War.

With the advent of artillery the story changed and Merle, being vulnerable to bombardment from the surrounding hills, was at last abandoned.

From here take the D136 and turn left onto the N120 to Le Relais du Teulet. After dinner return to watch the legend of Merle in 'Son et Lumière' which, with adjustments for the changing sunset times, continues through the Summer until the end of October.

Dinner and overnight accommodation at **Le Relais du Teulet**, Goulles.

L'Auberge des Ruines de Merle
St. Cirgues La Loutre
Tel: (55) 28 27 15

A charming little Auberge with pleasant rooms, a bar and a dining room with checked table cloths. Flowers grow in abundance around the terrace.

Simple well cooked country food.

Try 'Médaillon de pâté de foie' and 'charcuterie du pays' with a bottle of local wine.

Rooms: 9
Facilities: bar, restaurant, parking
Rating: ★★

Le Relais du Teulet
19430 Goulles
Tel: (55) 28 71 09

The Relais de Teulet is situated on the N 120 (not in the actual hamlet of Goulles) and is perhaps a little uninviting on first sight. It is a small, family-run inn with clean modest bedrooms. The restaurant, however, is large, attractive and rustically decorated. Here you will enjoy a wonderful regional dinner in the true French style; home-made soup will arrive in a large terrine and be ladled out at your table; follow this with your choice from one of their very reasonably priced menus, but be sure to finish with Madame's patisserie, coffee and brandy.

Food: Also refer to p. 136 for further specialities
Wine: Vin de Cahors
Rating: ★★

**ST. CIRGUES LA LOUTRE: USEFUL
INFORMATION**
Population: 267
Altitude: 460 metres

Hills Crowned with Castles

Château Castelnaud

DAY 5

From Goulles to La Roque Gageac.

Today following close to the river, which now flows through fertile pastures and walnut groves, you will travel down to the picturesque village, La Roque Gageac.

Make sure you travel with a jersey handy, for apart from viewing splendid châteaux and lunching on the terrace of the **Hostellerie Fénelon** in Carennac, you will visit the Grottes de La Cave; underground caves, with fairyland halls full of stalactites and stalagmites, which descend into the steep rocks beside the river.

Total mileage: 90.25 miles

Leave Goulles

After breakfast at Le Relais du Teulet take the N120/D12 via Argentat to Monçeaux.

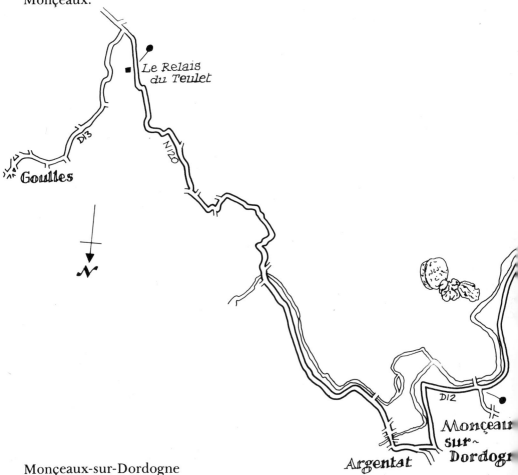

Monçeaux-sur-Dordogne

It really is worth while stopping here to look inside the picturesque country church. Its plain and simple exterior does not prepare you for the stunning interior with magnificent stained-glass windows and altars.

Continue on D12 to Beaulieu

From here the valley widens and passes through walnut groves to Beaulieu.

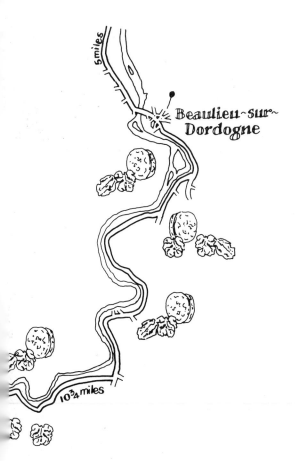

Beaulieu-sur-Dordogne

The Archbishop of Bourges visited this location in 855 and being enchanted by it he christened it 'Bellus Locus' 'Beaulieu', 'Beautiful place'.

Take time to walk down the quaint little streets to the river, and you will find this lovely town really does live up to its name.

A monastery quickly grew to considerable importance here, despite and during struggles over its suzerainty early in the twelfth century between the lords of Turene and Castlenau. The large Abbey church, L'Eglise de St. Pierre, was built by the monks of the Cluniac order in the twelfth century. The doorway was carved in 1125 by craftsmen from Toulouse, and is one of the greatest masterpieces of Romanesque sculpture, the theme on the Tympanum being 'The Last Judgement', dominated by Christ in the centre. It is to this fine Romanesque church of the former Benedictine monastery that Beaulieu owes its fame.

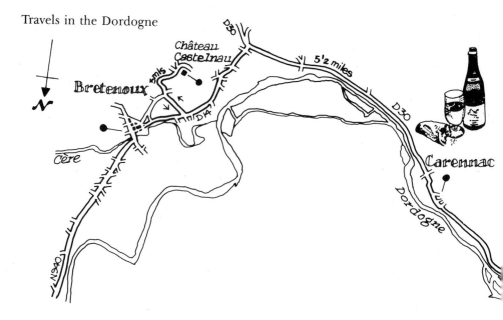

Under the onslaught of the Wars of Religion (1562–1598) the monks deserted the abbey, but in 1663 the abbot of La Tour d'Auvergne set upon its restoration and the community returned to live in serenity. It was the Revolution which finally drove the monks away.

Take the D940 to Bretenoux

Below Beaulieu the Dordogne slows down and winds through rich farmland to Bretenoux. X on the Cère

Bretenoux

This former bastide was founded in 1277 by the powerful Lord of Castelnau; it has conserved its grid plan and around the central square still stand the old houses and shops with their covered loggias.

Turn right onto the D14 to Château Castelnau

Château Castelnau

More than three miles around, the castle of Castelnau built of red iron-stone is a formidable example of medieval architecture, commanding the valleys of the Cère and the Dordogne.

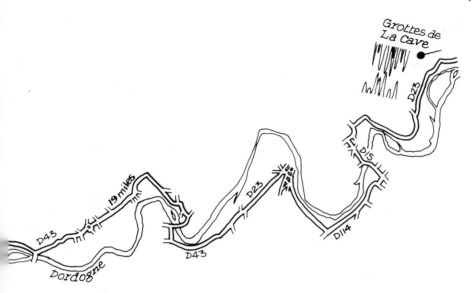

It was erected in the eleventh century and extended into a huge fortified fortress during the Hundred Years' War. The castle was abandoned in the eighteenth century, suffered badly during the Revolution, and finally was set on fire when the bankrupt owner wanted to collect on the insurance in 1850. However between 1896 and 1932 it was well-restored, much of the work being put through by Mouliérat — a tenor of the Opéra Comique — who brought it back to order and finally left it to the Nation.

In the court of honour stands the round keep and the impressive Saracen's Tower which is over 200 feet high, and gives one some idea of the vast scale of this fortress, whose garrison once numbered 1500 men and 100 horses. In the twelfth century the rent of one egg per year was carried with great ceremony by a yoke of 4 oxen to the overlord, the viscount of Turene.

Inside there are many interesting galleries to visit for their decoration and furnishing is very fine, much of it was collected by Mouliérat. The pewter hall and the grand salon contain Aubusson and Beauvais tapestries and the oratory has stained-glass windows from the fifteenth century.

Return to the D14 and then follow the D30 to Carennac.

Just downstream of Castelnau the river receives the waters of the Bave, and then the road follows the river on the left bank as it flows towards Carennac.

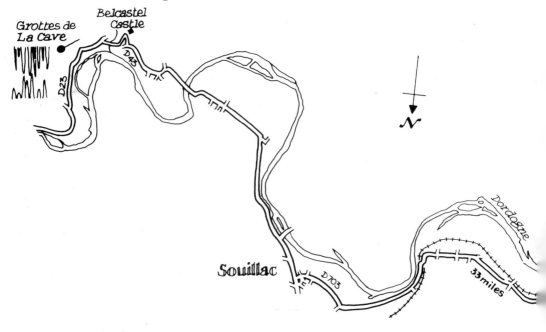

Carennac

Carennac is an attractive village, and the **Hostellerie Fénelon,** named after the famous writer who lived here, is a wonderful place in which to have lunch.

After lunch you can enjoy a relaxed walk around the enchanting houses with brown-tiled roofs, some dating from the sixteenth century, which cluster around the old Priory in which Fénelon once lived. Tradition has it that Fénelon wrote his masterpiece *Télémaque* in the tower which is named after him.

In front of the priory church, dedicated to St. Peter, is another fine carved porch, which would appear to belong to the same school as that at Beaulieu. The most outstanding item inside the church is the sixteenth century 'Placing In The Tomb'. Christ lies in a shroud held by two disciples, Joseph of Arimathaea and Nicodemus; at the back two women support the Virgin and the Apostle John: to the right Mary Magdalen wipes a tear.

From Carennac take the D43/D23/D114 and D23 to the Grottes de La Cave

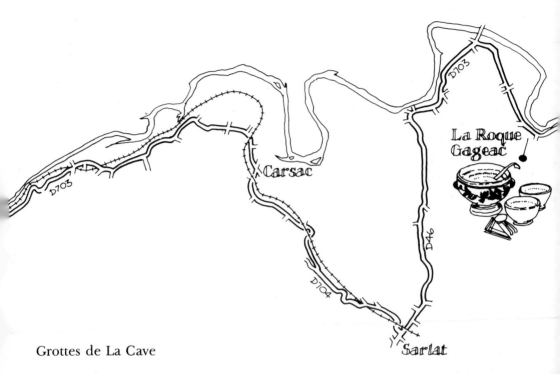

Grottes de La Cave

Having driven along the Dordogne through some very lovely scenery with good views of the river you will arrive at the famous caves of La Cave which were discovered in 1902 by Armand Viré. The twelve fairytale halls which have been galleried for visitors, are filled with stalactites and stalagmites of all shapes, sizes and colours forming astonishing reflections and mirages in the subterranean lakes.

Leave on the D43

Just past these caves on the top of a vertical cliff is Belcastel Castle. The chapel dates from the Middle Ages but most of the château was built during the last century. It is definitely worth stopping to take a stroll along the terrace, since from here there is a magnificent view of the junction of the river Ouysse and the Dordogne, even though the castle itself is not yet open to the public.

Return to the D43 and drive on through Souillac onto the D703 to Carsac, onto the D704 to Sarlat and then by the D46 and D703 to La Roque Gageac.

85

Travels in the Dordogne

La Roque Gageac

The picturesque village of La Roque Gageac is cut deep into the rocks beside the river. Little alleys, where peasant dwellings stand next to noble mansions, lead up to the church on the rock.

Wherever you walk you can't help being aware of the sheer cliff poised almost directly overhead, riddled with caves and bulging with precariously balanced pieces of rock. Indeed once, in 1956, a huge piece of rock did fall demolishing several buildings and causing loss of life; the patch of fresh surface where the rock split is still visible today.

Dinner and overnight at **Hotel Gardette**, La Roque Gageac.

La Roque Gageac

Hostellerie Fénelon
Carennac
46110 Vayrac
Tel:(65) 38 67 67
   (65) 38 47 16

The Hostellerie Fénelon is an adorable little hotel, roofed in brown tiles overlooking the River Dordogne and the Calypso Island. The terrace faces shaded greenery. It has a pretty dining room and excellent local cuisine cooked by the proprietor M. Guy Raynal.

The bedrooms are all attractively decorated and clean, and some rooms have a very good view over the river.

We found a very friendly ambience in this family-run inn.

Closed:	1st February to 15th March
Rooms:	22
Facilities:	bar, restaurant, function room, car park
	bathing and canoeing
Credit cards:	Visa
Food:	try the refreshing 'Assiette de Crudités' to start a light lunch
	(refer to p. 140 for other specialities)
Wine:	Try Vin de Glanes
Rating:	★★★

AUBERGE VIEUX QUERCY
46110 **Carennac**
Tel: (65) 38 47 01

A comfortable hotel/restaurant with good cuisine.

Closed:	15th December to 31st January
Rooms:	28
Credit cards:	Visa
Facilities:	bar, restaurant, car park

CARENNAC: USEFUL INFORMATION

Population: 400
Altitude: 126 metres
Sports: canoeing
        bathing
Facilities: hotels

**Hotel Gardette
La Roque Gageac
24250 Domme
Tel: (53) 29 51 58**

Perhaps our favourite of all the hotels/restaurants along the river; the ambience, cleanliness and cuisine were all faultless, not forgetting its idyllic setting in one of the prettiest villages in France overlooking the tranquil waters of the Dordogne. What more can I say, except that your stay here with the Gardette family will be quite delightful.

Closed: 15th October to 31st March
Rooms: 15
Facilities: bar, restaurant, terrace, car park, opposite
Credit cards: Visa
Food: try Filet de Boeuf aux cèpes
        (refer also to p. 143 for other specialities
Wine: try Bergerac blanc, Monbazillac and Vin de Noix
Rating: ★★★

LA ROQUE GAGEAC: USEFUL INFORMATION

Population: 373
Altitude: 150 metres
Sports: bathing
        angling
        canoeing
        walking
Facilities: camping site
        station at Sarlat, 8½ miles

DAY 6

Based at La Roque Gageac in the heart of the Dordogne, today's round trip
will encompass the fascinating town of Sarlat, where for the last week of July
and the first of August the market square becomes an open-air theatre with
performances of the classics (Shakespeare, Molière, etc.); the medieval city of
Domme, with lunch at the **Hotel L'Esplanade**, overlooking the valley; and in
the afternoon a visit to two very contrasting châteaux — the fairytale château
of Les Milandes, and the commanding twelfth century castle, Château
Castelnaud.

Total mileage: 34.25 miles

Château Les Milandes

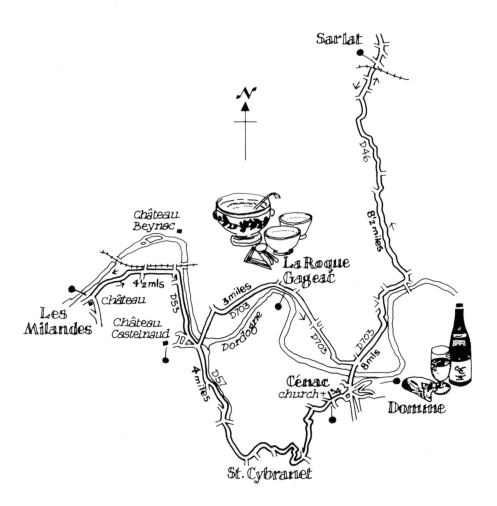

Leave La Roque Gageac

In the morning the sun's light will be glowing on the sandy coloured houses, and you will see why La Roque Gageac is considered to be one of the prettiest villages in France.

After breakfast take the D703/D46 to Sarlat.

90

Sarlat

Sarlat is the capital town of Périgord Noir (black perigord). Its narrow streets of ochre-coloured houses evoke the past when it was the home of merchants, scholars and law students. The charm of this attractive city has been enhanced since 1964 when restoration work began on a grand scale.

Sarlat was an episcopal seat from 1317–1790, and the Salignac Fénelon family ruled the diocese during the sixteenth century. The cathedral was built during the sixteenth and seventeenth centuries, although the belfry adjoining the west façade is undoubtedly romanesque.

Wander around behind the cathedral to find the Chapelle des Pénitents Bleus (twelfth century), the Cour des Fontaines and the Lanterne des Morts, a rather strange 12th century tower which was probably used as a funeral chapel.

If you are lucky enough to visit the city on a Saturday, it will be completely taken over by the market and in the 'Place des Oies' you will find the famous geese market — whose reputation spreads throughout France.

Take the D46/D703 across the Dordogne via Cénac and drive up the winding road to Domme.

Domme

Lunch at **Hotel de l'Esplanade**, Domme.

Situated on a huge rock overhanging the peaceful valley of the Dordogne stands the medieval city of Domme. This walled bastide which was built by the order of Philippe Le Hardi in 1281 can only be entered through three well-kept gates: the 'Del Bos', the 'Tower Gate' (Porte de la Tour), which was used as a prison from 1307–1318 and 'La Combe' which leads into the country.

Directly underneath Domme are its caves, which served as hiding places for the townspeople during the Hundred Years' War and then the Wars of Religion. Today they have been galleried and contain not only impressive crystallisations but also bones of bison and rhinocerous that were discovered during the excavations. The streets are narrow and steep and full of shops selling every gastronomic delicacy available in Périgord, see pp. 32–38.

The esplanade, known as La Barre, is the only part of the town which was not fortified when the city was built, because the sheer rock face beneath it was considered to be impregnable. However, in 1588, during the Wars of Religion, the famous protestant Captain Vivan scaled the face with thirty of his soldiers in the dead of night. His army was waiting outside the gates and in the confusion and rumpus the gates were opened and the town fell. Captain Vivan became master of the town until he rejoined the catholics in 1592.

Return to Cénac

Cénac Church

Below Domme is the village of Cénac, where there was once a large priory. The priory was destroyed by Captain Vivan during his exploits, but the small eleventh century Romanesque church, although greatly damaged during the Wars of Religion, still remains today. The original chevet, which can be seen in its full glory from the little churchyard, is the only section which was unharmed, the short nave and transept were rebuilt in the last century.

Leave the church and continue on D50 to St. Cybranet then take D57 to Castelnaud and D53 to Les Milandes.

Les Milandes

The pretty hamlet of Les Milandes is dominated by a fairytale château built in 1489. More recently the singer Josephine Baker, known in her Paris heyday in the Twenties and Thirties as La Perle Noire, made the château her 'Village of the world', thus proving that mutual understanding between different races need not be a Utopian dream.

The castle is surrounded by a beautifully landscaped garden.

Return by D53 to Castelnaud and drive to Château Castelnaud.

Château Castelnaud

The ruins of the Château Castelnaud are indeed impressive, commanding the valleys of the Céou and the Dordogne. In the twelfth century the castle belonged to the Cazenac family and at the time of the Albigensian crusade

(1209-1229) it was occupied by Simon de Montfort, father of the English statesman and soldier. In the fourteenth century the castle was fortified and was occupied for a considerable part of the Hundred Years' War, by the English. From here they were able to keep a close watch on neighbouring Château Beynac which was loyal to the King of France.

The panoramic view of the Dordogne from the east terrace is quite magnificent.

Return to the **Hotel Gardette** at La Roque Gageac D57/D703 for dinner.

Rue des Consuls, Sarlat

Hotel de L'Esplanade
Domme 24250
Dordogne
Tel: (53) 28 31 41

M. and Mme Gillard (he the chef, she the front of house manager), have refurbished this hotel which has always enjoyed a superb view. The rooms are all individually decorated in floral wallpapers in the true French rural tradition. The dining room is large and airy, and the food good, although sometimes a little expensive, but the portions are more than adequate.

Closed:	February and March
Rooms:	19
Facilities:	salon with TV, dining room, terrace with panoramic views
Credit cards:	American Express
Food:	fish and poultry excellent
Wine:	large wine list
	try local liqueurs
Rating:	★★★★

DOMME: USEFUL INFORMATION

Tourist Office:	50 Place Halle, Domme
	Tel: (53) 28 37 09
	Open 1st April to 15th October
Population:	891
Altitude:	212 metres
Sports:	bathing and canoeing at Cénac just below Domme on the River Dordogne
Facilities:	hotel
	camping
	aerodrome — excursions for tourists, most enjoyable mark my words
	best shops for gifts
Festivals:	1st September (or nearest Sunday) local fête with fireworks over the river

The Valley Widens

DAY 7

From La Roque Gageac to Bergerac.

Your first stop today is Château Beynac one of the most powerful castles in France in the Middle Ages, with superb views over the river, it was taken in 1195 by Richard the Lionheart. You will have lunch in a real fairytale château on the edge of the river at Lalinde, and then go on through the ever-widening valley full of tobacco fields to Bergerac.

Total mileage: 54.5 miles

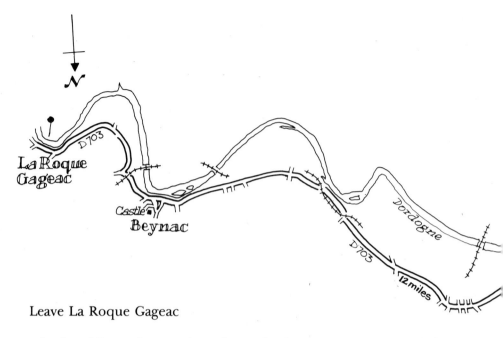

Leave La Roque Gageac

After breakfast at the Hotel Gardette take the D703 to Beynac and drive up to the castle.

Château Beynac

The formidable castle of Beynac rises from the top of a rock like an eagle's eyrie. Like Castelnaud, Beynac commands the valley of the Dordogne but from the opposite, north side of the river.

During the Hundred Years' War, when the Dordogne marked the frontier between the English and the French, there were constant skirmishes between them, but Beynac, protected by its double perimeter wall and its location on the steep rock face, remained unconquered.

Inside, the castle is being restored. The great hall of state, where once the nobles of Périgord used to meet, is decorated with gothic frescoes depicting the Last Supper. From the watchpath, which is reached by the main staircase, there is a breathtaking view of the Dordogne as it winds its way through the broadening valley to Lalinde.

Return to the village and take the D703 to Soirac-en-Périgord.

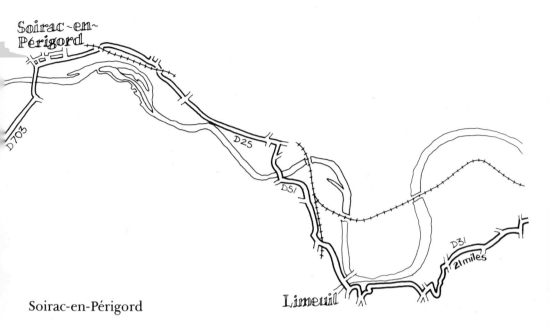

Soirac-en-Périgord

If you have a little time before continuing on to Lalinde for lunch, it is well worth visiting Madame Sarasin to buy some real Foie Gras to take home. Madame Sarasin will welcome you with open arms, guide you through her home to a large room where stands an impressive oak wardrobe bulging with this wonderful delicacy. You can even book dinner here 'Chez Famille' if you would like to experience real country fare. Directions can be obtained from the Tourist Office.

Take the D25/D51 to Limeuil, and then D31/D28/D29 and cross over the Dordogne into Lalinde.

Lalinde

Lalinde is a quiet town on the banks of the river.

The old château at the edge of the Dordogne is now a hotel and a first class restaurant offering an admirable place to stop for lunch and admire the river.

Leave Lalinde by crossing back over the river and take the D29/D37 to Lanquais.

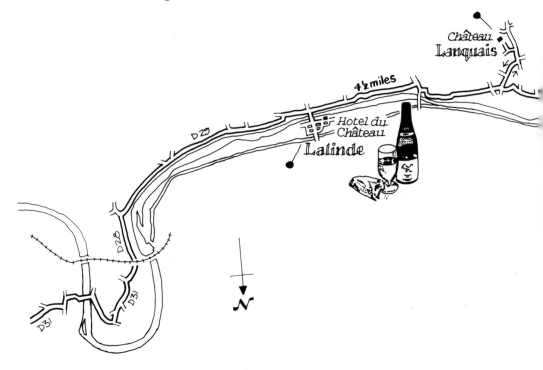

Château Lanquais

This castle is unusual in that it was built over a long period in many architectural styles, the renaissance hall was added on to the original gothic tower.

During the Hundred Years' War its inhabitants the Lacropte family were first allied to the English and then to the French.

The castle flourished during the Renaissance, when the large hall was built. Inside this hall are the most beautiful lacey stone fireplaces carved by Italian sculptors, who also worked at the Louvre in Paris. The tour of the castle ends in the kitchens where amid the cooking paraphernalia the flavour of Périgord lingers on.

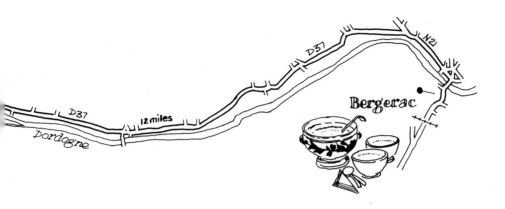

From Lanquais take the D37/N21 to Bergerac, cross over the river and continue on the N21 towards Périgueux to the Hotel La Flambée outside Bergerac.

Dinner and overnight at the **Hotel La Flambée**.

Hotel-Restaurant du Château
Rue de Verdun
24150 **Lalinde-en-Périgord**
Tel: (53) 61 01 82

Lunch in a real château on the banks of the river, this is the Restaurant du Château. The surroundings are romantic and the food good. Friends of ours travel out from Bergerac for dinner here. Marie Claude and Guy Gensou will give you a warm welcome.

Hotel La Flambée
Route de Pombonne
Bergerac 24100
Tel: (53) 57 52 33

This is a lovely comfortable hotel situated 3 km outside Bergerac in large grounds.

M. Bournizel the proprietor will not only make you welcome but wine and dine you to match. The menu contains amongst other things, local specialities — for example confit d'oie and foie gras. We were recommended by M. Daniel Lopez from Bergerac, and were well pleased in all respects.

Closed:	2nd to 22nd January
	9th to 24th June
Rooms:	21
Facilities:	bar, restaurant, tennis, large grounds, parking
Credit cards:	American Express, Diners Club, Access, Visa
Food:	being in Périgord why not treat yourself to truffles
Wine:	House excellent, good cellar also
Rating:	★★★★

LE CYRANO
2 bd Montaigne
Bergerac
Tel: (53) 57 05 13

Don't be put off by the outside of this hotel/restaurant, for inside the decor is superb. Jean-Paul Turon, owner and chef, has continued running Le Cyrano after his father. The food is of good quality, but unfortunately has a tendency to follow the 'nouvelle cuisine' method, a fashion which I am glad to say will shortly die.

Closed: 27th June to 12th July
                     4th to 27th December
Rooms: 11
Facilities: bar, restaurant, lounge, car park at rear
Credit cards: American Express
Food: fish terrine or mousse excellent
Wine: try Bergerac wines which are mostly underestimated in
                     England
Rating: ★★★

BERGERAC: USEFUL INFORMATION

Tourist Office: 97 Rue Neuve d'Argenson
                     Tel: (53) 57 03 11
Population: 28,617
Facilities: hotels
                     restaurants
                     camping sites
                     airport
                     station
Market day: generally Saturday mornings

Château Monbazillac

DAY 8

Based at Bergerac in the heart of wine country a short drive through acres of vineyards will take you to the famous Château Monbazillac, which houses exhibits of wine-making and local Protestant history. Here, the grapes are allowed to ripen to 'noble rot' producing a sweet white wine.

For lunch in the château restaurant, Pâté Foie Gras with Monbazillac wine is a must here. After lunch drive back to Bergerac and explore this well-restored town on foot.

Total mileage: 14 miles

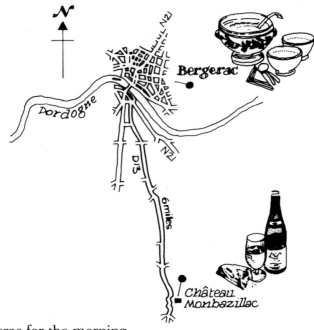

Leave Bergerac for the morning.

After breakfasting at the Hotel Flambée drive out to Château Monbazillac on N21/D13.

Château Monbazillac and lunch in Château Restaurant

The famous Château Monbazillac, just a few miles to the south of Bergerac, has a reputation which goes back hundreds of years; for the vineyards of this elegant château have produced excellent wine ever since the Middle Ages.

Legend has it that in older days when pilgrims from Bergerac were visiting Rome, the Pope asked, 'where is Bergerac?'; and the chamberlain replied, 'well, it is near Monbazillac'.

Today the château is run as a co-operative, but its wine is still the best of the appellations within Bergerac, even though it is no longer made by hand and foot in the original laborious way.

The neatly tended vineyards stretch out for miles around, and on a clear day one can see Bergerac in the distance. The bunches of white grapes are picked when they are very ripe and have a high sugar content, the stage known as 'noble rot', a guarantee that the wine will be of the quality expected.

After wandering around this picturesque château and enjoying lunch in its restaurant drive back to Bergerac and park near the church of Notre Dame.

Take the D13/N21 back to Bergerac.

Bergerac

Bergerac is the largest and most important town in the southern Dordogne, being the local centre for agriculture, wine and tobacco.

The old town begins below the beautiful gothic-style church and runs down towards the river, and so I suggest you take a little promenade to view the interesting sites which, despite the destructive effects of the Hundred Years' War (when the Earl of Derby took it), repeated during the Religious Wars, and natural depradations of time, have now been restored to their former glory.

The gothic-style church of Notre Dame, was built in the sixteenth century and has a slender bell tower, a wonderful organ and a wealth of stained-glass windows.

The covered market is built on the site of an old temple which was destroyed in 1682. In the north-west corner of the square above the little grocer's shop are a corner turret and gable, the only remains of the house in which Charles IX and his mother Catherine de Medici lodged in 1565.

In the Place Pelissière at the foot of the Grand Rue stands L'Eglise de St. Jacques with its ancient arched belfry, where in the Middle Ages pilgrims bound for Compostella used to stop.

Near by you will find the Museum of Sacred Art.

Behind the square in the Rue des Fontaines stands 'La Vielle Auberge' (the old inn) which is reputed to be the oldest house in Bergerac. It has now been authentically restored by its owner Daniel Lopez who will be pleased to show you around.

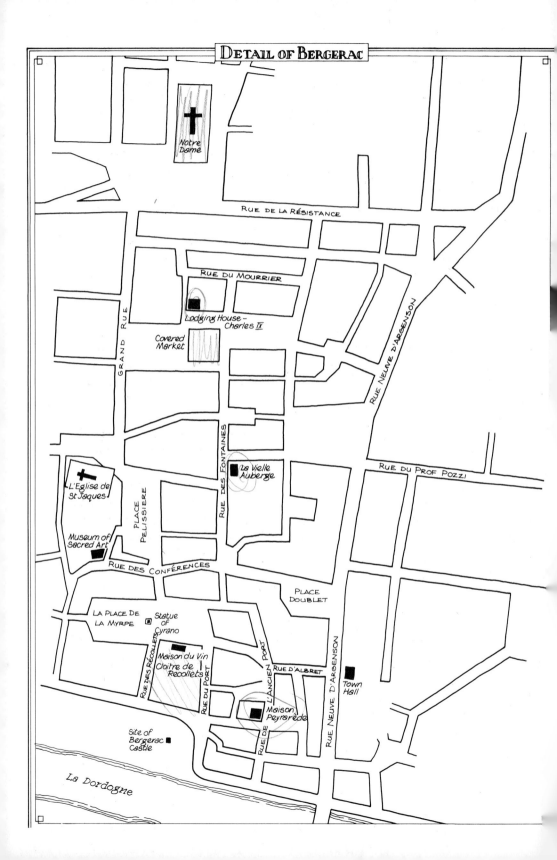

In the square, La Place de la Myrpe, bordered by many little old houses some still of wattle and daub, stands a statue of Cyrano, the fictional character created by the writer Edmond Rostand.

Close by is the Maison du Vin and Cloitre de Recollets. This monastery is now the interprofessional council for Bergerac wines, which has renovated the buildings. They are definitely worth a visit, because, from a meeting room on the first floor, there is a view of the river and the vineyards of Monbazillac.

By the quay on the site of the original wharves, once stood Bergerac castle. It was flanked by two ports to which barges brought timber from the Auvergne and from which the wines of Bergerac and Monbazillac were shipped to England and the Netherlands.

The Maison Peyrarède, faces the Rue de l'Ancien Port. It is an interesting fifteenth century building which was extensively altered in 1603, presumably to make it ready for the arrival of Louis XIII who stayed there in 1621. Today it houses the only tobacco museum in France, and contains some very interesting exhibits.

You will have passed by many tobacco fields already so you will not be surprised to learn that it plays a major part in the economy of Périgord.

The climate in south-west France is extremely favourable for this plant, which was first imported from America in the sixteenth century, ironically, for medicinal purposes. Harvesting is done stem by stem. The stems are then hung upside down in airy sheds to dry for about six weeks, before they are sent to a central warehouse for processing.

At the end of the Rue D'Albret is the Hotel de Ville (town hall). Once a convent, then a hospital, it became the town hall in 1904.

From here I suggest you wander slowly back to your car, but on the way take time to digest this lovely town by having an aperitif in one of the numerous cafés before you return to the **Hotel La Flambée** for dinner.

Return to **Hotel La Flambée** for dinner and overnight.

Vines As Far As The Eye Can See

DAY 9

From Bergerac to St. Emilion.

The drive from Bergerac to St. Emilion will take you across the wide alluvial plains of the Dordogne valley, along straight roads bordered by vineyards. If the harvest has started, do stop to watch and sample the freshly picked grapes. Leave some room for a leisurely lunch in Castillon and then amble on to St. Emilion and the 'pièce de résistance' of your hotels the **Hostellerie de Plaisance**.

Total distance: 35 miles

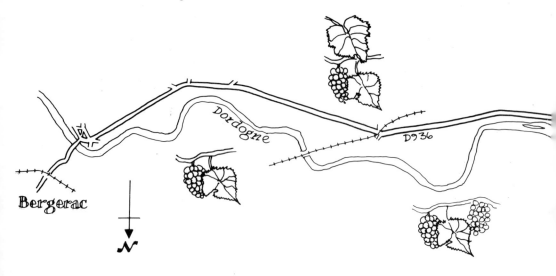

Leave Bergerac.

After breakfast at the Hotel La Flambée take the D936 along the south bank of the river to St. Foy La Grande, and then cross over to the north side and continue on the D936 to Castillon-La-Bataille.

Castillon-La-Bataille

From Bergerac the Dordogne follows its ever-wider valley, now bordered by acres of vineyards to Castillon-La-Bataille.

Castillon is a busy town on the north bank of the river. It was here in 1453 that the English, under the aged Sir John Talbot, were defeated by the French King's army. After the battle, the town, not at all pleased at being rescued from the English, was ransacked by the French. Talbot was killed and there is a small monument to him alongside the river. This major defeat led to the evacuation of the English from the whole of France except Calais, and so marked the end of the Hundred Years' War.

Lunch at **La Bonne Auberge**.

Take the D936 towards Libourne turning right to St. Emilion, (signposted) to the Hostellerie de Plaisance.

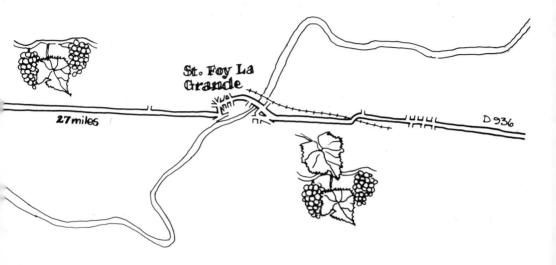

St. Emilion

Arrive at **Hostellerie de Plaisance.**

I suggest you prepare for the evening in a leisurely manner. The atmosphere of the town can best be sampled with an aperitif beneath the acacia tree in the square below the hotel.

Dinner and overnight at **Hostellerie de Plaisance**, St. Emilion.

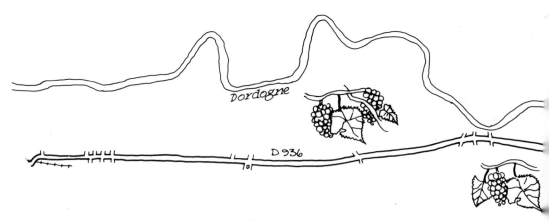

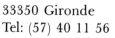

La Bonne Auberge
12 Rue du 8 Mai
Castillon-La-Bataille
33350 Gironde
Tel: (57) 40 11 56

Have lunch on the terrace or in the picturesque courtyard under parasols. A much-loved restaurant by the French (always a good recommendation).

If you wish to stay it has 10 pleasant bedrooms, but closes from the 2nd to the 20th November.

Rating: ★★★

CASTILLON-LA-BATAILLE: USEFUL INFORMATION

Tourist Office:	Hôtel de Ville, Central Square
Population:	3207
Altitude:	20 metres
Sports:	swimming
	tennis
	fishing
Facilities:	hotels
	camping
Festivals:	large celebrations at Easter and Pentecost

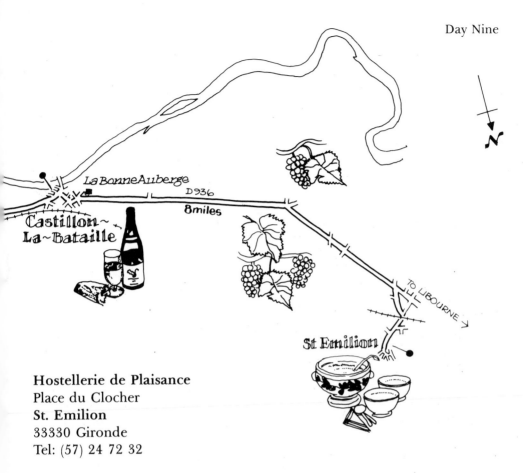

Hostellerie de Plaisance
Place du Clocher
St. Emilion
33330 Gironde
Tel: (57) 24 72 32

A *very luxurious hotel* which is considered to be one of the best in this part of France. Its setting above the church in this sleepy unspoilt town is quite unique. Sit and sip aperitifs on the terrace looking out over St. Emilion and the Dordogne valley; and after a gourmet dinner retire to the bedroom of your choice for a welcome sleep.

Rooms:	12 suites/rooms
Facilities:	bar, restaurant and terrace
Credit cards:	American Express, Diners Club, Access, Visa
Food:	try mussel soup, and meat cooked in old local wine
Wine:	St. Emilion, of course
Rating:	★★★★★

For alternative accommodation and Useful Information for St. Emilion, see p. 119.

St. Emilion

DAY 10

St. Emilion
Your chance to explore the place which is not only a town but a vintage. The centre of the most celebrated of wine districts around Bordeaux. For lunch I would strongly recommend the **Logis de La Cadène**, Place Marché-au-Bois, but hold back on the wine, for in the afternoon you can take a 'dégustation' at the Château de Roques.

View St. Emilion.

Macaroons are a speciality here, sample them whilst walking through the streets.

St. Emilion is a sleepy wine town steeped in character, a rural gem of Bordelais. St. Emilion was founded by St. Emilione as a hermitage as long ago as the eighth century. The town is Roman in origin, it is built on two hills from where across the rooftops one can see the valley of the Dordogne, and the rich vineyards which produce some of the most famous wines in France.

It was fortified in the days of Henry II (Plantagenet), and ruins of some of the original ramparts can still be seen today.

Following a charter given by John Lackland in 1199, the parish of St. Emilion was administered by a council known as the Jurade right up until 1790.

Even today the Jurade, now an elite committee, has a role to play. Every year in spring, the Jurats don their red robes trimmed with ermine and attend mass. After this ceremony each château can submit its wine from the previous year, now ageing in oak barrels, for judgement. Only then, if the Jurade consider it to be of the highest quality will it gain the honour of holding the label 'St. Emilion appellation contrôlée'.

In late September, again dressed in full regalia, the Jurade process through the streets of St. Emilion to the Kings Tower, which was built in 1224, from where the 'Premier Jurat' proclaims that the harvest may begin.

There are many historical monuments to visit here, even though, like so many towns St. Emilion was hard hit during the Hundred Years' War.

The collegiate church in which, on the 10th March, 1310, the dukedom of Guyene was restored to the King of England, Edward the First, is one of the largest in the Gironde, and has fine stained-glass windows donated by Louis XII.

The 9th century monolithic church, underneath your hotel, is unique in France, as you will appreciate when you see it. Its steeple was built in the twelfth, fifteenth and sixteenth centuries.

It is also worth wandering through the streets up to the elegant cordelier cloisters to partake of a glass of wine or methode champagnoise, whilst admiring the well preserved 15th century church.

In the afternoon you may like to visit the cellars of Château de Roques (visits in English) and enjoy a dégustation, and even purchase some wine. See map below for directions.

Return to the **Hostellerie de Plaisance.**

Dinner and overnight at **Hostellerie de Plaisance.**

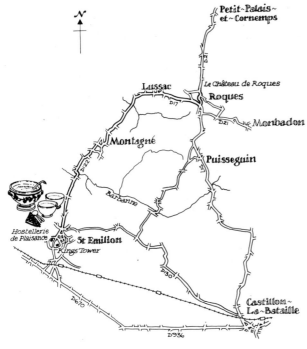

AUBERGE DE LA COMMANDERIE
Rue Cordeliers
St. Emilion
33330 Gironde
Tel: (57) 24 70 19

A much smaller and modest hotel with 15 rooms. Stay here if you wish, but try to eat at the Hostellerie de Plaisance.

Rating: ★★★

Logis de La Cadène
Place Marché-au-Bois
St. Emilion
33330 Gironde
Tel: (57) 24 71 40

An eighteenth century house with a warm and friendly atmosphere. The cooking has a family style.

ST. EMILION: USEFUL INFORMATION

Tourist Office:	Place du Clocher
	Tel: (57) 24 72 03
Population:	3000
Altitude:	102 metres
Sports:	horse riding
Facilities:	hotels
	camping
	wine tasting
Festivals:	2nd Sunday in June — Fête de La Jurade
	3rd Sunday in September — Ban des Vendanges de La Jurade de St. Emilion

The Journey Ends

St. Emilion

DAY 11

St. Emilion to Blaye

Today's excursion takes you to your final destination, Blaye. You will visit Libourne which was founded as a bastide in 1265 by the English seneschal, Roger de Leyburn, and named Libournia after him, lunch at the restaurant Cartagène in St. André de Cubzac, and then drive on to the sleepy village of Bourg, which was producing wine long before the mighty Médoc was even planted. Just a few miles from here, the Dordogne merges with the river Garonne to form the estuary of La Gironde. You will see this junction clearly from the pretty coast road — for Innes and I this was a moment of great nostalgia. Drive on to the citadel at Blaye to your hotel and a delicious dinner.

Total mileage: 38.5 miles

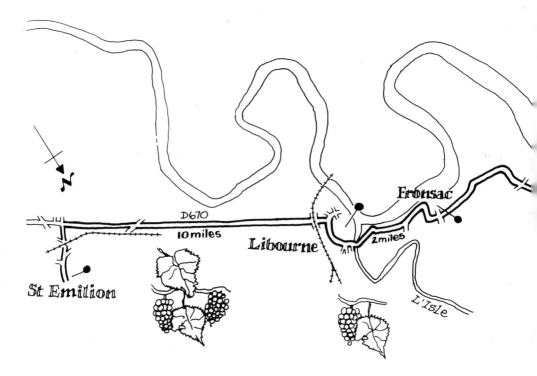

Leave St. Emilion.

After breakfast in the Hostellerie de Plaisance leave St. Emilion and return to the main D670 to Libourne.

Libourne

Libourne was built under English occupation at the end of the thirteenth century around a central square. The town hall was built in 1429 and has been carefully restored. Where the Dordogne meets the river Isle, there was once a large port for the export of wine. The wine was brought down the rivers on gabares (flat-bottomed boats), which were then broken up to make wine casks. Today it is still a market centre for the local wines of St. Emilion, Pomerol and Fronsac.

Bordering the river Isle stands the Tour du Grand Port, the last surviving witness of the old line of fortifications which once protected Libourne from invasion.

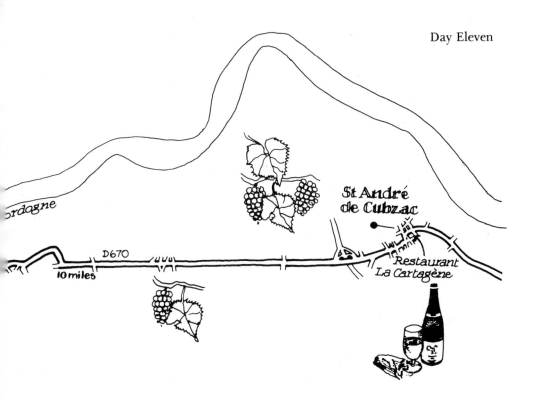

From here the D670 runs on the right bank of the river to Fronsac.

Fronsac

The little village of Fronsac is proud of its one-thousand-year-old vineyard. The knoll — a source of local pride — is crowned by its romantic church, offering a wonderful view of Libourne, the river Isle and the Dordogne.

Take the D670 which runs through acres of vineyards to St. André de Cubzac.

Lunch at **Restaurant Le Cartagène**, St. André de Cubzac.

After lunch take the D670/D669 to Bourg-sur-Gironde.

Bourg

Only the shortage of reasonably priced good wines has forced people to re-explore this area which makes true clarets for everyday drinking. The best

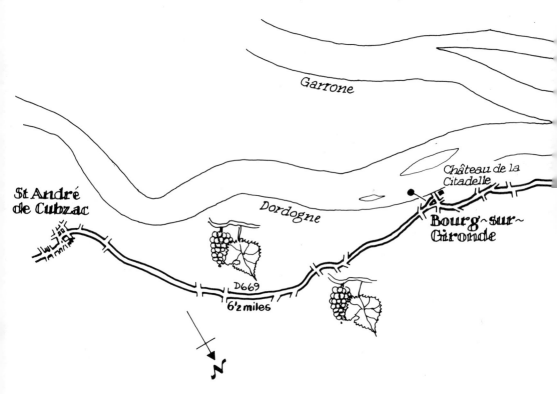

châteaux of Bousquet and Tayac produce wines which are not only good when young, but will age excellently.

Bourg itself is a quaint little town situated on the edge of the river in an area surrounded by irregular soft hills. It is divided into two; the lower ancient port no longer in use, and the upper town inside the ruins of the old fortifications. The lower and upper parts are joined by a steep stone staircase which passes under a medieval archway.

In the centre of the town is the attractive Victoriana covered market, which comes to life early on a Sunday morning. The eighteenth century Château de la Citadelle was once the summer residence of the Archbishop of Bordeaux. Now it is usually empty, although it is sometimes used for meetings. It has been restored and is surrounded by lovely gardens.

From the terrace you will be able to look at the Dordogne for the last time, for it is only a few miles from this château that the Dordogne and the Garonne converge.

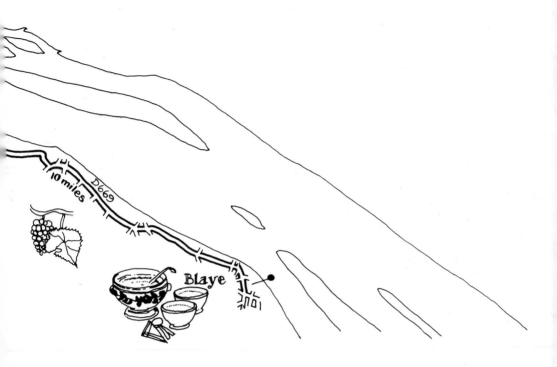

Take the Route Touristique D669/D669E/D669 to Blaye.

Below Bourg the road winds along the pretty coastline of the estuary, through villages and vineyards until it finally arrives at your journey's end in the walled and moated seventeenth century citadel of Blaye.

Blaye

Dinner and overnight inside the citadel at the **Hotel de la Citadelle**.

Restaurant le Cartegène,
187 rue Nationale
Place du Champ de Foire
33240 **St. André de Cubzac**
Tel: (57) 43 20 42

An unassuming and delightful little restaurant with a pretty terrace and garden behind. All the dishes are carefully cooked here, but do try their home-produced pâté de foie de canard, (duck pâté) with a bottle of Côte de Bourg (red wine) to wash it down — quite delicious.

Hotel de la Citadelle
Dans La Citadelle
Blaye
33390 Gironde
Tel: (57) 42 17 10

A first class modern hotel situated within the city walls, with magnificent views over the estuary of La Gironde. The bedrooms are all smartly decorated and most look out onto the hotel's heated swimming pool. A very convenient spot for seeping up the history of Blaye, and relaxing before your homeward journey.

Good service and excellent cuisine.

Rooms:	21
Facilities:	lounge, bar, restaurant, conference room, parking, swimming pool
Credit cards:	American Express, Diners Club, Visa
Food:	try Lotte à l'Armoricaine and Magret de Canard (refer also to p. 146 for other specialities)
Wine:	try Côte de Blaye
Rating:	★★★★

BLAYE: USEFUL INFORMATION	
Tourist Office:	Allées Marines
	Tel: (57) 42 02 45
Population:	4800
Altitude:	8 metres
Sports:	tennis
	horse-riding
	swimming
	estuary fishing
Facilities:	hotel
	camping
Market day:	Saturday morning

Blaye

DAY 12

Discover Blaye on foot. The Romans were the first to garrison Blaye which, from its height on the right bank of the Gironde, commands the point where the river broadens into the estuary. Two towers of the medieval Château des Rudel remain, as well as a legend. It concerns Jaufré Rudel, a twelfth century troubadour, who fell in love, sight unseen, with the Princess Mélisande of Tripoli, and finally sailed to see her only to die in her arms on landing.

Early evening take a stroll around the seventeenth century battlements and enjoy the most magnificent sunset in the whole of France.

Blaye

After breakfast it is well worth walking around the old citadel and indeed the town of Blaye.

Below Blaye the Gironde opens out into an estuary 6 miles wide, so any tide-bourne invader trying to attack Bordeaux would have found the channel opposite Blaye narrowing to no less than one mile.

Blaye has always been an important defensive post and inevitably changed hands in the long medieval struggle between the English and the French.

Apart from the ruins of the twelfth century Château des Rudel, little remains, for in 1689 Vauban, Louis XIV's great military engineer, cleared the town to make way for the citadel which you see today. A house in its centre was the prison, from November 1832 to May 1833, of the widowed Marie-Caroline, Duchess of Berry, whose husband was a younger brother of the guillotined Louis XVI. In an attempt to dethrone King Louis-Philippe in favour of her posthumous son, the Comte de Chambord, last of the Bourbon line, she engineered an uprising in the Vendée. It was quelled and the duchess's credit was destroyed when she gave birth to a daughter, few believed the tale she told of a secret marriage.

The low town is comparatively modern. A deep water basin accommodates small cargo ships and fishing vessels which bring in sturgeon, lamphreys and fish.

The estuary has been dredged to allow the passage of deep water tankers to the two large refineries on the islands.

The other two bastions which completed Vauban's defensive barrier are the Fort Paté on the small island opposite Blaye and Fort Médoc on the far bank of the estuary.

So the Dordogne has reached its destination and you have followed its course from its tiny source high up in the mountains of Mont-Dore, through the gorges of the Auvergne, across the wide alluvial plains of Périgord, through perhaps some of the most breathtaking scenery in France to its mouth — the estuary of La Gironde, from where it flows out into the Atlantic Ocean.

I do hope you have enjoyed your holiday and will go home to try out the recipes that follow from some great chefs.

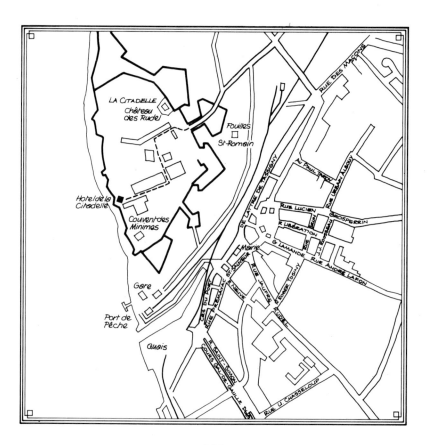

Recipes From The Region

MENU 1 ⚜

by Alain Cosnefroy Chef/Owner of **Le Relais Arverne**, Saignes (Auvergne).

Alain Cosnefroy was born in 1955 in Caen. After studying to be a chef for three years, he worked in restaurants from Toulouse to Paris, before opening this excellent Hotel/Restaurant with his wife in Saignes. This hotel is highly recommended in the *Logis de France*.

Salade Auvergnate
A dressed green salad with smoked ham, cheese and nuts

. . .

Coquille de Moule à la Niçoise
A cocktail of mussels presented in a scallop shell

. . .

Pavé Grillé au Bleu D'Auvergne
Fillet of beef with Cognac and herbs

. . .

Wine suggestion — St. Pourçain Red or Red Bordeaux

. . .

Fromage
Fourme D'Ambert

. . .

Dessert
Délice du Relais Arverne
Vanilla ice cream with rum, chantilly and chestnut purée

Salade Auvergnate

1 lettuce finely shredded
16 oz smoked french
ham sliced into julienne
strips
16 oz blue cheese
(preferably Fourme
D'Ambert) chopped
into small cubes
1 packet of chopped
mixed nuts
8 tomatoes cut into
1/6ths
½ cucumber sliced
Home-made french
vinaigrette dressing
garnish: parsley

For 8 persons

A dressed green salad with smoked ham, cheese and nuts.

Place a bed of shredded lettuce into 8 individual salad bowls. Arrange the other ingredients artistically on the lettuce pour over the vinaigrette dressing and garnish with fresh parsley.

Coquille de Moule à la Niçoise

4 pints mussels*
4 hard boiled eggs
7 oz tin of tuna fish
Small tin of anchovy
fillets
2½ ozs small black olives
½ onion finely chopped
½ lettuce finely shredded
4 tomatoes finely
chopped
Home made french
garlic dressing
8 scallop shells
garnish: parsley

For 8 persons

A cocktail of mussels presented in a scallop shell

* Clean mussels thoroughly. Put a little white wine (½ pint) and pepper into a large pan, bring to the boil. Add the mussels, cover and cook briskly for 5–10 minutes until open. Remove mussels from the pan and shell, but discard any which do not open. (The liquid can be used for a fish soup if desired.)

Toss the lettuce and onions in the dressing and place a small amount into each scallop shell. Toss the mussels, tuna and chopped tomato in the dressing and place on top of the lettuce leaving enough room in the centre for ½ a hard boiled egg. Criss-cross the anchovy fillets over the egg and dot around the olives. Top with a little more vinaigrette and garnish with parsley.

Pavé Grillé au Bleu D'Auvergne

Fillet of beef with cognac and herbs

8 6–8 oz portions of
fillet steak
Butter for frying
Salt, pepper and mixed
herbs for seasoning
Cognac
8 oz cheese — Bleu
d'Auvergne or similar
½ pint double cream
garnish: parsley sprigs

For 8 persons

Melt the butter in a skillet, fry the fillets with seasoning to taste until cooked to the required amount; add a little cognac and the double cream. Place a piece of cheese on the top of each fillet, put under a hot grill until browned. Serve immediately with a little sauce and garnish with parsley sprigs.

Délice du Relais Arverne

Vanilla ice cream with rum, chantilly and chestnut purée

1½–2 pints of home
made or best vanilla ice
cream
½ tin of chestnut purée
mixed with ½ pint of
single cream and rum
until soft
1 pint of chantilly
cream
4 oz black chocolate
grated

For 8 persons

Place the vanilla ice cream in layers with the rum and chestnut purée in a tall glass with lashing of chantilly cream and grated chocolate. (Chantilly — whipped cream slightly sweetened and flavoured with vanilla.)

"Relais Arverne"

MENU 2 ⚜

by Yvonne Clavières and A.M. Marty, Le Relais du Teulet, Goulles (Auvergne).

This small coaching inn is a family run concern situated on the RN 120. The bedrooms are modest but the cuisine is excellent.

Purée de Carotte
Cream of carrot soup

. . .

Ris de Veau sur Canapé
Veal sweetbreads in a wine and cream sauce served on croutons

. . .

Civet de Lièvre
A rich casserole of hare

. . .

Wine suggestion — Red from Cahors

. . .

Fromage
Bleu D'Auvergne

. . .

Dessert
Tarte de Cassis
Blackcurrant tart

Purée de Carotte

Cream of carrot soup

2 lb carrots sliced
4 sticks celery chopped
2 large onions chopped
2 oz butter
2 tbls oil
2½ pints chicken stock
1 bay leaf
grated rind and juice of
1 orange
½ pt double cream
salt and pepper
garnish: chopped fresh
chives

For 8 persons

Fry carrots, celery and onions gently in the butter and oil for 5–10 minutes, stirring occasionally. Add stock, bay leaf, orange rind and juice and seasoning. Bring to the boil, cover and simmer for 25–30 minutes. Remove bay leaf, liquidise and return soup to pan. Add cream, taste for seasoning, bring just to the boil and serve sprinkled with chopped chives.

Ris de Veau sur Canapé

Veal sweetbreads in a wine and cream sauce served on croutons

2 lb calves or lambs
sweetbreads
3½ pints water
6 oz onions peeled and
sliced
Bouquet garni
Salt and 6 peppercorns
4 oz butter
Black pepper
7 tablespoons white
wine
¼ pint double cream
2 apples cored and
sliced
1 tablespoon potato
flour
garnish: 8 large
croutons (canapés) of
fried bread, chopped
parsley and sliced fresh
apple rings

For 8 persons

Make a stock of water, onions, the bouquet garni, 1 teaspoon salt and 6 peppercorns, and simmer in a large saucepan for 30 minutes. Blanch the sweetbreads in the liquid for 20 minutes over a low heat. Strain, reserving a teacup of stock, and place the sweetbreads in a bowl of cold water. When cold remove the membrane and dry.

Melt 2 oz of butter in a large frying pan. Add the sweetbreads and when firm but not coloured, add salt and pepper, cover and leave simmering for 20 minutes.

Then add the white wine, double cream and 3 tablespoons of stock, mix well, bring to simmering point, draw pan from heat, cover and leave to macerate for 10 minutes.

Cook the apples in the remaining butter until they are tender.

Remove the sweetbreads from the pan with a slotted spoon.

Mix the potato flour with cold water until smooth. Whisk it into the sauce a teaspoon at a time over the heat until the sauce is creamy and thick. Add the sweetbreads and apples.

Serve on croutons garnished with apple rings and chopped parsley.

Civet de Lièvre

1 hare — 4–5 lb in weight
2 onions
½ bottle red wine
3 shallots
6 oz streaky bacon
½ lb mushrooms
1 clove garlic
32 button onions glazed in butter
1 bunch chervil and parsley
1 glass brandy
3 oz butter
1 oz plain flour

For 8 persons

A rich casserole of hare

Order the hare already jointed from your butcher, but ask him to include the blood with the order.

Chop the bacon, vegetables and herbs and fry with the butter and hare in a large heavy based saucepan until brown. Add the wine and brandy to cover the meat and vegetables. Cover the pan and cook over a slow heat for 2½–3 hours or until tender. Mix flour into a smooth paste and add to stew; cook for 2–3 minutes more. Remove the pan from heat and stir in the blood. Serve with croutons.

Tarte de Cassis

10 inch diameter tart tin
8 oz flour
4 oz butter cut into
small pieces
3 oz granulated sugar
pinch of salt
1 medium egg
1½ lbs blackcurrants
and 4 oz blackcurrant
jelly

For 8 persons

Blackcurrant tart

Sift flour on to paper and set aside.

Drop pieces of butter into a warm mixing bowl, add sugar and salt and work together until creamy, (use wooden spatula). Break in the egg and work until smooth. Pour in the sifted flour, mix well. Put the pastry on to a floured board and work the ingredients lightly with the fingers until a ball forms. Cut pastry into 4 pieces, pile one on top of the other and push them down firmly. Do this 3 times. Leave to rest for at least 1 hour before use.

Heat oven to 220°C, 425°F or Gas 7. Roll out pastry and line the buttered and floured tart tin. Trim pastry leaving ¼ inch above the edge of the tin. Prick the base and chill for 30 minutes. Fill the case with 1½ lbs of blackcurrants. Bake for 20 minutes then reduce heat to 160°C, 325°F or Gas 4, and cook for further 20–25 minutes. Take out to cool.

Melt 4 oz blackcurrant jelly, and when the tart is cold brush the fruit and pastry edge with it, pouring remainder over fruit.

Serve with fresh cream.

139

MENU 3 ⚜

by Guy Raynal Chef/Owner of **Hostellerie Fénelon**,
Carennac (Périgord).

Guy Raynal was born in 1946 and studied to be a
chef at the Hotel du Touring at St. Cère. After
working locally in Souillac and high up in the Alps in
Izère, the Raynal family purchased the Hostellerie
Fénelon in 1974.

Melon au Cassis
Melon filled with blackcurrant liqueur

. . .

Truite Farcie aux Ecrevisses
Trout stuffed with succulent prawns

. . .

Confit D'Oie aux Cèpes
*Goose cooked in the traditional Périgordian manner
served with cèpe mushrooms and wine*

. . .

**Wine suggestion — Vin de Glanes or
Vin de Cahors**

. . .

Fromage
Fromage de noix

. . .

Dessert
Coupe aux vieille prune
Vanilla ice cream, chantilly cream and prune liqueur

Melon au Cassis

4 charentais melons
1 bottle of Crème de
Cassis

For 8 persons

Melon filled with blackcurrant liqueur

Cut the melons in half and scoop out the pips. Serve in glass dishes filling the holes with Crème de Cassis.

Truite Farcie aux Ecrevisses

8 7 oz trout
8 oz butter
8 oz peeled prawns
salt and black pepper
8 tsps. chopped tarragon
mixed with 1 tsp. dried
thyme
Melted butter for
coating
garnish: lemon, whole
prawns, parsley

For 8 persons

Trout stuffed with prawns

Clean, scale, wash and dry the trout thoroughly.

Mix together the butter, seasoning, herbs and prawns to a paste. Stuff the inside of the trout and sew up the fish with cotton. Brush the trout with melted butter and place on an oiled grill rack, cover and bake for 35–40 minutes until tender.

To serve cut away the cotton and decorate with lemon, whole prawns and parsley.

Confit D'Oie aux Cèpes

Confit d'oie Périgourdine
(preserved goose)

1 10–12 lb goose
enough salt to rub all
the pieces
¼ pint cold water

For 8 persons

Goose cooked in the traditional Périgordian manner served with cèpe mushrooms and wine.

Cut the goose into pieces. Cut away all the fat from the inside and reserve. If there is not enough fat use pork or beef dripping later on. Rub the pieces of goose all over with salt. Leave for 24 hours.

Melt the fat, add the pieces of goose plus the

141

water. Cover the pot and simmer very slowly for 3 hours.

Sprinkle salt inside a deep glazed jar or basin, pour in some fat; when set add the goose and cover completely with the rest of the fat. Store in a cool place. This will keep for months until required.

For confit d'oie aux cèpes.
Dig out the goose and heat up in its fat with plenty of cèpe mushrooms and wine.

Coupe aux Vieille Prune

1½–2 pints of home made or best vanilla ice cream
1 pint of chantilly cream
1 large jar of prunes in armagnac

For 8 persons

Vanilla ice cream, chantilly cream and prune liqueur.

Place scoops of ice cream in large glasses, put in plenty of prunes and armagnac; top with chantilly cream.

MENU 4 ⚜

by Jean Jacques Bourmier Chef-Owner of **Hotel Gardette**, La Roque Gageac, Domme (Périgord).

Jean Bourmier studied to be a chef in St. Yvieix 'Haute Vienne', and then worked in the Hilton, Stratford-on-Avon, the Plein Ciel Hilton, Brussels and the Framtel in Limoges. He married Mme. Gardette's daughter and has become a valued member of the Gardette family.

Pâté de Foie Gras
Served with toast and Monbazillac wine

. . .

Salade Périgourdine
Lettuce, haricots verts, confit d'oie and truffles in a nut oil dressing

. . .

Poularde aux Champignons et ses Nouilles Fraiches
Chicken cooked with cream and mushrooms, served with fresh buttered noodles

. . .

Wine suggestion — Bergerac Blanc

. . .

Fromage
Trappe

. . .

Dessert
Patisserie Maison
Fresh strawberry gateau

Pâté de Foie Gras

Served with Monbazillac wine

It is almost impossible to obtain the correct goose livers to make this pâté in England, so it is suggested that you buy a good 100% Foie Gras and a Château Monbazillac wine, and devour it with your friends on your return to England!

Salade Périgourdine

1 lettuce finely shredded
1 lb haricot verts — cooked lightly and cooled
1 lb meat from the confit d'oie (cold) — chopped (p. 141)
Walnut oil vinaigrette
Sliced truffles to 'bank balance' for garnish (alternative sliced flat mushrooms)

For 8 persons

Lettuce, haricot verts, confit d'oie and truffles in a nut oil dressing.

Place a bed of shredded lettuce into 8 individual salad bowls. Toss the other ingredients (except for the truffles) in plenty of walnut oil dressing and arrange in a pile on the lettuce. Garnish with criss-crosses of truffle.

Poularde aux Champignons et ses Nouilles Fraiches

2 chickens
4 onions
4 sticks celery
3 oz unsalted butter
Salt and black pepper
2 bay leaves
32 button mushrooms
2 teaspoons Dijon mustard
2 level tablespoons plain flour

Chicken cooked with cream and mushrooms, served with fresh buttered noodles.

Chop the celery and onions finely. Melt 2 oz of the butter in a very large, heavy pan; sauté the celery and onion until soft. Put the chickens, giblets and liver in the pan with the celery and onion with enough water to cover the chickens. Bring to the boil, skim and add salt, pepper and bay leaves. Cover the pan and simmer for about 1½ hours or until the chicken is tender.

5 fluid oz double cream
16 oz fresh buttered
noodles
garnish: 2 tablespoons
of finely chopped
parsley

For 8 persons

Take the chickens out and keep them warm. Strain the stock and keep. Slice the mushrooms and cook in the remaining butter for 2–3 minutes. Sieve the flour over the mushrooms, and cook stirring continuously; gradually blend in about ½ pint of the stock and the cream to make a smooth sauce. Add the mustard and extra seasoning to taste.

Carve the chicken into joints, arrange in a deep serving dish and pour the sauce over. Sprinkle with chopped parsley and serve with buttered noodles.

Patisserie Maison

4 eggs
4 oz caster sugar
4 oz self raising flour
¼ level teaspoon salt
¾ lb fresh strawberries
½ pint double cream
3 oz icing sugar

For 8 persons

Fresh strawberry gateau

Grease and flour a rectangular tin about 14 in x 8 in. Whisk the eggs and caster sugar together until they are pale and thick. Sift the flour and salt, and fold into the egg mixture. Spoon the mixture into the prepared tin. Bake for 15 minutes or until it is golden brown and firm to the touch, just above the centre of a pre-heated oven at 375°F or Gas mark 5.

Turn the sponge out on to a rack to cool. Whip the cream until thick and fluffy.

Cut the sponge in half, place one half on a plate and cover with cream and sliced strawberries; slice the other half into two layers and cover each layer with cream and strawberries. Finally, sprinkle with icing sugar.

This makes a very exotic three-tiered dessert.

MENU 5 ⚜

by M. W. Schaer Chef de Cuisine, **Hotel La Citadelle,** Blaye (Gironde).

A very comfortable hotel within the ancient citadel walls of Blaye. Lunch can be taken around the attractive swimming pool. Excellent cuisine.

Les Huitres 'Marenne'
½ dozen Marenne oysters with lemon and vinegar

. . .

Cuisses de Grenouilles Sautées Fines Herbes
Frogs legs sautéed with butter and herbs

. . .

Filet de Boeuf en Croute
Fillet of beef with pâté in puff pastry

. . .

Wine suggestion — Château de Bousquet Côte de Bourg

. . .

Fromage
Roquefort

. . .

Dessert
Sorbet de fraises et de framboises
Strawberry and raspberry sorbet

Les Huitres 'Marenne'

Allow 6 oysters per person

Open just before serving and place the oyster still in its shell on a bed of crushed ice. Garnish with lemon segments and thin brown bread and butter.

Cuisses de Grenouilles Sautées Fines Herbes

Allow 6–8 frogs legs per person and serve with french bread.

Frogs legs sautéed with butter and herbs.

Fry the frogs legs in hot butter with chopped parsley, crushed garlic and lemon juice.

Filet de Boeuf en Croute

1 fillet of beef (4 lb approximately)
1 lb strong pâté with mushrooms (or truffled pâté de foie gras)
2½ lb puff pastry
Madeira sauce (see below)
1 egg yolk
Butter
garnish: plenty of fresh watercress

For 8 persons

Fillet of beef with pâté in puff pastry.

Cover the meat with a generous layer of butter, season, brown and partially cook the fillet in a hot oven 450°F or Gas 8 about 20 minutes. Allow to cool. Spread the meat with pâté and wrap up in the pastry. Place seam side down on a baking sheet. Decorate with strips of pastry or shapes and prick to allow the steam to escape. Brush with milk. Cook in a hot oven 425° or Gas 7 until the pastry is golden brown. Decorate with watercress, carve at the table and serve with Madeira sauce.

Madeira Sauce

2½ oz flour
4 oz butter
⅔ pint home-made beef bouillon

Melt the 4 oz butter in a thick based saucepan. Add the flour, beat in and cook for 1 minute. Pour in the bouillon little by little whisking

147

⅓ pint Madeira
1 oz caster sugar
Salt and pepper
½ oz butter chopped
into very small pieces

continuously, then still whisking add the Madeira, sugar and salt and pepper to taste.

Continue stirring and cook until the sauce has reduced and thickened. The consistency should be of single cream.

Before serving add the small pieces of butter.

Sorbet de Fraises et de Framboises

1½ lb strawberries
(fresh)
1½ lb raspberries (fresh)

10½ oz sugar
¾ pint water
Juice of 3 lemons

For 8 persons

Strawberry and raspberry sorbet

Hull the fruit, mash or liquidise and pass through a fine sieve to remove the pips. Beat in the sugar thoroughly, add water and strained lemon juice.

Pour into container and freeze for 1 hour. Remove, beat with a fork and refreeze for 4 hours (longer if necessary).

Serve in elegant glasses.

Selected Bibliography

A Regional Geography of Western Europe (4th edition), F.J. Monkhouse, Longman, London, 1974.

France its Geography and Growth, Jean Dollfus, trs. John Patterson, Murray, London, 1969.

The World Atlas of Wine (rev. edition), Hugh Johnson, Mitchell Beazley, London, 1977.

France, John P. Harris, Macmillan, London, 1986. Well worth buying and reading before you travel.

Geographical Index

Index of Recipes

Glossary of Food Terms

Starters

charcuterie	cold meats (pork)
crudités	raw vegetables
escargots	snails
potage	soup
terrine	less finely chopped pâté

Meats (Viande)

agneau (gigot de)	lamb (leg of)
boeuf (filet de)	beef (fillet steak)
bleu	very rare
saignant	rare
à point	medium
bien cuit	well done
brochette	kebab
côte/côtelette	chop
entrecôte	steak (rib)
jambon	ham
lapin	rabbit
lièvre	hare
mouton	mutton
saucisse	sausage (fresh)
saucisson	sausage (dry)
veau	veal

Offal (Abats)

boudin	black pudding
cervelle	brains
foie	liver
langue	tongue
ris	sweetbreads
rognon	kidney

Poultry (Volaille) and Game (Gibier)

caille	quail
canard/caneton	duck/duckling
coq	cockerel
faisan	pheasant
oie	goose
perdrix	partridge

pintade	guinea fowl
poulet	chicken
sanglier	wild boar

Fish (Poisson) and Shellfish (Crustacés/Coquillages)

alose	shad
anguilles (en gelée)	eels (jellied)
bouquet	prawn
brochet	pike
cabillaud	cod
Coquilles St. Jacques	scallops
crevettes	prawns/shrimps
écrevisse	crayfish
fruits de mer	mixed shellfish
hareng	herring
homard	lobster
huitres	oysters
langoustine	scampi
lamproie	lamphrey
lotte	monkfish
loup de mer	sea bass
maquereau	mackerel
moules	mussels
saumon	salmon
truite	trout

Vegetables (Légumes)

ail	garlic
artichaut	artichoke (globe)
asperge	asparagus
carotte	carrot
champignon	mushroom
chou	cabbage
choucroute	sauerkraut
choufleur	cauliflower
épinards	spinach
haricots verts	French beans
navet	turnip
oignon	onion
pomme de terre	potato
au four	baked, roast
purée	mashed
petits pois	peas
poireau	leek
poivron	green/red pepper
riz	rice

Fruit

ananas	pineapples
cassis	blackcurrant
cerise	cherry
citron	lemon
fraise	strawberry
framboise	raspberry
groseille	redcurrant
mur	blackberry
pamplemousse	grapefruit
pêche	peach
poire	pear
pomme	apple
prune	plum

SETTING UP IN FRANCE

For everyone who is interested in buying, leasing,
renting or time-sharing in France.

This book will cover everything from raising
the money to installing water, gas, electricity,
planning permissions and much more in urban and
rural sites throughout France.

* * * * * * * *

Written by Laetitia de Warren, the French born
editor of Le Magazine, this will become 'the'
reference book on the subject.

Available May 1987 from booksellers at £8.95
or direct from the publisher at £8.95 plus £1.15
post and packing.

OTHER PHOENIX TRAVEL TITLES

Travels in Provence	April 1987
Travels in Normandy	September 1987
Travels in Brittany	September 1987
Travels in the Loire	Spring 1988
Travels in Alsace	Spring 1988
Travels in Burgundy	Spring 1988